scm centrebooks

KU-705-145

David Jenkins

What is Man?

SCM PRESS LTD

334 01781 5
First published 1970
by SCM Press Ltd
56 Bloomsbury Street London WC 1
© *SCM Press Ltd 1970*
Printed in Great Britain by
Billing & Sons Limited
Guildford and London

Contents

1 The Question of the Question

Rhinoceroses have always fascinated me. They are quite unbelievable but they exist. They certainly exist because you can see them at the zoo. Consider what they actually look like if you gaze at one of them in a corner of a paddock and look unhurriedly and carefully. Their skin apparently does not fit. It is wrinkled, baggy and arranged in folds. At one end of the animal is a stick-like tail with exiguous bristles of hair. At the head end it is difficult to decide which is more odd, the square elongated outline of the muzzle if you imagine the horns not there, or the general effect if you take it all in, complete with scimitar-like appendages sticking upwards and sometimes seeming to force the animal to carry its head low because of the size and weight. The eyes certainly show that this shapeless and uncontrolled shape is alive, but they seem to be of the wrong size and in the wrong place. The ears have their outline pricked out in bristles, and if you catch them set forward in a lively angle you can almost bring yourself to believe that the whole animal of which they are a part does make sense – until you glance again over the shambling and unbalanced effect.

The odd and the exciting thing about a rhinoceros is that it exists, it is there. I do not find my sense of oddity or excitment assuaged by a description, however illuminating or interesting, of the ecological niche which the rhinoceros family has found for itself in the bush or savannah country of Africa. This provides a context for its oddness, but it is still *there* in its odd way – that of being a rhinoceros. Nor is the exciting oddness removed by an account, however detailed and fascinating, of the evolutionary development of these quadrupeds which, accidentally, look so reptilian. It helps me, in a way, to see how they came to be what they are. But the really odd and exciting thing remains *that* they are – like this. My problem is not solved.

But I am not quite sure that it is a *problem*. In the feeling of

7

oddity and of excitement, there is, certainly, an element of raising a question. It is almost as if I was wanting to ask the question 'Why this?' and 'Why this like this?'. But on reflection, it is not clear to me that I am really raising these questions, or, at least, that if I am raising these questions I am not expecting answers to them. Rather, the questioning attitude is like a raising of the eyebrows which is part of my expression of the enjoyment, wonder and interest that I feel at being presented with this sort of existence and existing. The fascinating point about the rhinoceros is that there it is as a rhinoceros. What I really enjoy is the experience of reacting to its existence by the feeling that it ought not to exist like that. But I am not really asking for someone to explain to me just why it exists like that so that all the oddness goes away. To explain the existence of the rhinoceros as a rhinoceros in such a way that I was freed from all perception of oddness or all puzzlement about incongruity would certainly be to explain away my enjoyment of and reaction to the rhinoceros. I am also inclined to the view that, in an odd sort of way, it would explain away the rhinoceros too, or, at least, reduce its existence as a rhinoceros to a matter of total indifference.

It may be that the reader has never seen a rhinoceros, or has seen one but finds it just one more of the sorts of creatures we come across which are all odd if you look at them in one way, but, really, there is nothing odd in their oddness. There just is a variety of animals, as of other phenomena. Basically this is not odd but just so. If this is your position about, or reaction to, what I have been so far trying to draw attention to, then I presume that you find nothing particularly interesting or significant in putting or considering the question 'What is a rhinoceros?'. It is simply a question for information put by somebody who has heard the word used and wants to know what the word refers to. The curiosity implied by the question does not go very far and is soon satisfied. For example, it will be satisfied as soon as someone shows the questioner a picture of a rhinoceros or takes him to the part of the zoo where a living one can be seen. If the questioner is 'interested in animals' then he may want a good book or article, i.e., something that gives him some accurate zoological information, but once he has enough information that will be that. There is nothing mysterious, odd or exciting about a rhinoceros or about a rhinoceros being a rhinoceros. There is just a case of ignorance to be removed.

Is the question 'What is man?' just like the question 'What is a rhinoceros?' taken in this latter way? Or, to put it another way round, if we ask the question 'What is man?', what sort of question are we asking, why are we asking it and what sorts of answers would satisfy us, would remove the problem or problems which provoked the question? Or should we, even, be satisfied if the problem were removed? It might be that the attitude, response and reaction involved in asking the question 'What is man?' is much nearer to what I have been trying to describe in referring to my reactions to a rhinoceros. That is, the question may be much more indicative of our interest, wonder, puzzlement, enjoyment and bewilderment about being a man and being confronted with men, rather than being a request for nothing but information which would 'settle' the question. Would you be satisfied with an answer to the question 'What is man?' which finally stopped you wanting to ask the question? Do you think that it would be 'a good thing' if you *were* satisfied? Might it even be a 'good thing' (whatever that means) to try to get people who had never dreamed of asking the question 'What is man?' to start asking it?

We might perhaps get further enlightenment on the oddness and possible importance of this question 'What is man?' if we consider that the question about the rhinoceros would not be phrased 'What is rhinoceros?', but 'What is *a* rhinoceros?'. In English as we customarily use it, the first form of the question does not quite make sense, or at least, we are not sure what the sense is. The second form makes sense, and we know what sorts of answers, giving what sorts of information, would be answers to that question. I have been trying to suggest, however, that my reaction to the existence of a rhinoceros as a rhinoceros has an element in it which is not satisfied by, is even liable to be disappointed by, mere information about *a* rhinoceros. My attitude and reflection might perhaps be better symbolized after all by the question 'What is rhinoceros?'. However, the people who find the existence of rhinoceroses totally uninteresting would think that a silly question. The rest of us would not find it easy to say what the question meant, so I am inclined to follow up my clue touched on earlier and ask whether it is basically a question at all. I wonder whether what is wanted is not a symbol like 'What a rhinoceros'*!* (exclamation, *not* question) or 'Oh, rhinoceros!'.

On the other hand, the whole business of curiosity and even excitement, of raising a question or being forced to an exclamation, starts from encountering *a* rhinoceros. The initial provocation to whatever one is provoked to arises from a particular experience of a particular animal and example of the species. Perhaps, therefore, in trying to consider the nature and bearing of the question 'What is man?', we should consider the question 'What is *a* man?'. But this question does not have the same 'feel' as the question 'What is a rhinoceros?'. The question about a rhinoceros can be plausibly disposed of by a certain amount of information or by pointing to a rhinoceros. Indeed, there will be many people who feel that my whole attempt to suggest that there is *more* to being a rhinoceros than that is rather far-fetched and fanciful. But I suggest that scarcely anyone will feel that it is plausible or satisfactory to dispose of the question 'What is a man?' like that.

For example, let us suppose that some piece of space-fiction comes true and that some planet in a different galaxy has a zoo in it. It announces that it has a very rare and recently captured exhibit – a man. Some young planetling reads the notice and remarks electronically, 'Daddy, what is a man?'. The answer is now simple. Father and planetling go to the zoo and the youngster is told, 'There is a man'.

But is that all there is to be said? Even if it were supplemented by a computer-compiled brochure on the habits and earthly environment of the species man, would it be enough? Most of us would think not (or, at least, *feel* not), even if many of us begin to suspect or fear that, provided the information collecting and scanning was broad enough and the programming of the computer accurate enough, then the planetary electronic brochure might contain all that is to be said. What, then, is the point or bearing of this feeling that the 'zoo-type' answer to the question is not enough, and what is the nature of the fear that we might have to become persuaded that it is, after all, all that can or should be said?

Consider further these two pictures of a rhinoceros in a paddock and a man in a planetary zoo. A rhinoceros is – a rhinoceros, even if the zoo authorities have given him (? it) a name. A man, however, is – not primarily a man, but himself! To refer to this feature of being a man we use (not very precise) words like 'individual' and 'person'. We do not think of members of the human species whom

10

we personally know simply and primarily as examples of the human species with certain specific distinguishing characteristics, but we think of them by their 'proper names'; that is, we think of them as selves, and as themselves. To think of a man or a woman not as a self but as an object-like example of the species is a shocking violation of what we find most important and human about those men and women *we know*. (We shall have to consider at a later stage in our discussion how we are to face the fact (? threat) that we do seem brutally capable of treating human beings as mere objects in a variety of ways and circumstances.) A man, therefore, is not just a man; he is himself, he is a self. To ask the question 'What is a man?' is just the same as to ask the question 'What is man?'. We are expressing our wonder, puzzlement, bewilderment, hope about what we are up against here.

More than this, we are, of course, asking about *ourselves*, for we know that we are men and our direct experience of what it is to be a self is confined to our individual experiences of being ourselves. The question 'What is man?' is therefore very closely related to, if it is not actually the same as, the question 'Who am I?'. This, I fancy, at once makes it clear why we feel that what I have called the 'zoo-type' answer to the question is not enough, and why we fear being compelled to accept as a fact that we are capable of being exhaustively described and classified. If, as men, we really belong in the same categories of classification and description as can be given to all the animals in the zoo, then our uniqueness is gone. And it is not merely our uniqueness as a race which is gone; it is our uniqueness as ourselves. For there is only one 'I' (me!), and the only way for it really to be meaningful that I am 'me' is that it should truly be the case that I am unique, i.e., primarily *my* self and not basically simply a case of the species man.

In fact we have, I think, stumbled across a profitable focus for considering our question 'What is man?'. It is to be found in the issue of the uniqueness of man.

Indeed, it is pretty clear that to ask the question 'What is man?', in so far as it is really a question and not just an exclamation and expression of puzzlement, wonderment or worry, is at least to enquire into what is *different* about being a man. What distinguishes a man from any other sort of animal or other existence there is? What is it that it is particularly important to take into account in dealing with men, or of having hope of men, or making plans for men? What is there about being a man which puts him or her before me as a human being and not a mere block of shaped flesh, an ape or an angel?

I think that in the formulation of the last three questions we can perhaps begin to see a clue (which must be followed up later) as to why we are unable to decide whether our question is really a question or something more like an exclamation. In so far as we are looking for marks of difference we are looking for defining and distinctive characteristics, and we want *information* about these. Information answers questions. But the information we want is connected with hopes, plans and aims. And hopes, plans and aims are connected with notions and experiences like fulfilment, worthwhileness, enjoyment. In *this* realm (of enjoying being what one is, where one is or where one is going and the like) it is not information which is really important, but experience. Satisfying experience does not answer questions, it renders them irrelevant or else it provokes further questions, or perhaps better, further questings.

For example, we may be provoked to curiosity by the fact that someone gives up all his spare time in working for, say, mentally handicapped children. To find out 'Why?', we can acquire information about our friend's character and circumstances, about the conditions and circumstances of handicapped children and about the details of what is done with them and for them. We shall not, however, *understand* what our friend is up to unless and until we catch at least a glimpse of 'what it feels like' to be both helped and to be helping, to be cared for and to be caring. This shared experience renders our search for information irrelevant by replacing it, although it may well set us off on a further quest which will involve both questions about and questing into being able to care and being in need of care. We need to bear in mind through the rest of our discussion that the question 'What is man?' is almost certainly only partly a question looking for information which would 'answer' it. It is also quite possibly an exclamation reflecting the experience of questing, seeking, being unsatisfied and satisfied which is involved in being a man. We shall also have to consider what is the relation between information we are given about the human species and the experience and questing of being a man. Bearing this in mind, we can return to this issue of the uniqueness of man which, I am suggesting, can serve as a useful focus for opening out our inquiry.

I am further suggesting that on the face of it we can see the uniqueness of man lying in the existence of ourselves as selves, that is as having an awareness of our existence as being something that is our own. This awareness seems to be unique in a twofold sense. First, we do not know of any other species of animal that has it and, secondly, it is an awareness of uniqueness, that is, an awareness that I am me and not anyone or anything else. I wish to put the weight of our investigatory argument on this second aspect of the uniqueness, viz. that I am a self-reflecting animal who is aware that I am me. My main reason for doing this is what I consider to be a practical rather than a theoretical one, namely that if the question 'What is man?' is considered at all, it will be considered by individuals who are concerned about what it is to be themselves in relation to other selves. The ultimate conclusion of the investigation may be that being a self is *not* significant. But being a self, knowing about this and wondering about this is the starting point. So here we have a *prima facie* experienced uniqueness to begin from.

Beginning from this experience of (apparent) uniqueness frees us, at this stage of the argument at least, from the need of discussing whether self-consciousness really is unique (i.e., as a matter of fact not found anywhere else than in man). Man's continuity as a species with animal life in general and the interesting popularity of books stressing this continuity and arguing that we must understand ourselves basically in terms of this continuity (as, e.g., naked apes) will be discussed later. At the moment I am simple making our way into facing the question 'What is man?' by following up the clue of our experience of ourselves as selves, an experience which involves an apparent experience of our own individual uniqueness. 'What is man?' is involved with the question 'What am I'? and the experience of being an 'I' involves at least an apparent experience of uniqueness. To deny the existence of this uniqueness by e.g. treating *a* man like *a* rhinoceros (of the planetary zoo) is shocking to us (although this does not prevent shocking behaviour to men by men), and to have this uniqueness threatened by the apparent likelihood of it being possible to give a computerized description which conveys all the information there is about the human species is also threatening and frightening to us.

The question 'What is man?' is thus an odd question (like or unlike the question 'What is a rhinoceros?'?), and an oddly important question. It is not at all clear that it is just a question, or that information could or would settle it. It is seeking to focus our attention and reflection on the experience of being a man, and it rather suggests that this experience itself involves questings and questionings. As all this is odd and complex, and seemingly leads to piling questions on questions, could we not, after all, avoid asking the question?

It does not seem very likely that we could. Two broadly obvious facts about the human species to date are that man is a religion-producing animal and that he is an art and, eventually, literature-producing animal. Religion may be on the way out because God is finished and about to be finished with, but on any interpretation religion is a powerful witness to man's apparently inveterate habit of wondering about himself, about his place in the scheme of things, about his relation to what there is and might be, about the 'meaning' of his existence. What religion so powerfully witnesses to, art or / and literature in every age, including very definitely this one, underlines. Man is an object of endless fascination, concern, worry, enjoyment, despair, frustration and hope to himself. Past and present performance and history therefore suggest that men neither can nor will stop asking the question 'What is man?'.

Before, however, we proceed to explore the possibility of a viable and distinctive Christian way of facing this perennial question we should consider what I take as a growing feeling and suggestion that we *ought* to stop asking it, at least in the ways hitherto typical of religion, philosophy and literature. I deduce this challenge to the whole of our previous ways of considering the question particularly from the growing evidence that articulate young people throughout the world are focusing on one concern and one concern only, that of society. Their reactions and their efforts seem to be directed either to reforming society or to dropping out of society. Moreover, the reform which is sought is as sharp and as drastic as is implied by the complementary reaction of 'dropping out'. Society has to be changed in a drastic, in a revolutionary, way.

The point that I want to focus on here is not the rightness or wrongness of particular forms of protest, or of particular things that are protested against. Nor do I want, if I can avoid it, to contribute to the romantic idealization of youth, or middle-aged envy and fear of them. An adolescent identity-crisis is an adolescent identity-crisis whether it happens to be privately experienced or publicly and corporately enjoyed, whether it is violently expressed or privately wrestled with. But the present question is whether the particular forms and manifestations of the protests and pretensions of the young we are now experiencing are not so violent and so widespread for a particular reason. Is it that the hitherto accepted shapes and identities of our society and societies are now felt to be particularly questionable and particularly to be questioned? And that this questioning is directed very sharply to the very area which we are trying to work out as our area of inquiry?

Thus, I am suggesting that it looks as if men have always asked 'What is man?', that this is an odd fact about man itself, and that the question is an odd sort of question. It looks like a request for information, and one would suppose that information is relevant to 'answering' the question. We shall have to spend a good deal of time in the rest of the book considering how information about, e.g., the animal nature of man, the psychological determinism of man, the social and cultural conditioning of man, affects and ought to affect our view of the answer to our question 'What is man?'. On the other hand, the question is almost certainly not just a request for information. Or alternatively, the information which could *satisfactorily* answer the question is an odd sort of information.

This is because the question turns out to focus on questions like 'Who am I?', 'What does it mean to me to be a "self"?', or even, 'What would it mean to discover a satisfactory meaning for being one?'!! It is at this point that we see why the question has to be considered also as an exclamation, an exclamation which, I have hinted, might be 'satisfied' by an experience, but is not just like a question which can be disposed of by an answer. I do not know whether my rhinoceros has turned out for most readers to be a rather bulky and tedious red-herring. Perhaps it is sheer donnish perverseness to try and use discussion of a rhinoceros to attempt to evoke a sense of how exciting it can be to be. My trouble, doubtless, is that I would like to be a poet but I have no gift for it. This much, however, might be said at this stage. It looks as if 'What is man?' is a scientific question. It turns out that 'What is man?' is much more like a poetic question/exclamation. But I, at any rate, refuse to allow poetry and science to fall apart or be totally opposed to one another. This may be because I am incapable of being a poet and have not been trained to be a scientist. I am going to go on writing this book on the much more hopeful hypothesis that it is because I am a man, a reflective self-conscious animal who invents science and thinks up (?feels up – ?or . . . ?) poetry.

But – I got to this recapitulation of where I felt my arguings or wonderings had so far reached in my attempt to confront 'the youth protest'. For all my reflections are attempts to pick up the relevant resonance of scientific, philosophical and poetical questionings which are of the nature of internal monologues and soliloquies about 'What is man?', 'Who am I?', 'What does it *mean* to be a self?'. The question that I hear as one of the articulate and pointed questions to be detected in the babel of protest is the question posed to all this tradition of reflection and self-examination. As I hear this question it takes a form like, 'But have you not reflected that all these reflections of the self-conscious society, of men who display acute sensibilities as to the meaning of being themselves, are in practice, the manifestations of the insensitive society?' The self-conscious society is the insensitive society. The thousand and one ways of asking the question 'What is man?' are not only luxuries, but drugs, designed, however unknowingly, to spare us the need, and the opportunity, of living as men with men for men.

It may be that Marx was needed to remind philosophers that the human job is not to think about reality but to change it and that now we need various forms of protest and drop-out to remind us that the human job is not basically, and certainly not exclusively, to think about reality or change reality, but to live it. It may not be at all clear what I am trying to say here, but it should be borne in mind that there are two possible reasons for my being on the verge of nonsense. The first is that I am indulging in vague and romantic word-spinning, which cannot be eventually brought to evoke significance because it is just word-spinning and not a responsible attempt to respond to something really but vaguely seen, and which demands working at until clarification is achieved. The second reason is that my imprecision, with its threats of nonsense, arises because I am trying to draw attention to something which is sensibly and sensitively inviting us to consider whether the threat of nonsense does not lie in what we have settled down to regard as determinative of sense.

The question of nonsense is not a nonsense question. The people who drop out of society may be making nonsense of society. Certainly society thinks so, for it wishes to suppress them, tidy them up and get them out of the way. Drop-outs are to be treated with aggressiveness and contempt which barely conceals hate and fear. But society may already be pretty good nonsense, in which case the drop-outs are making very good sense. They may perhaps be (doubtless, very often despite themselves) the latest version of the child who *says* that the emperor has no clothes. (We have pretty high authority for associating a child's insight with the kingdom of heaven. And while men have always tamed Jesus and his kingdom in their concepts, they have never stopped the effects of his unexpectedness for long.)

My main initial reasons for holding that we must give heed to these protests in this sort of way are as follows. First, it becomes clearer and clearer to me that so much of what 'adult society' takes seriously for granted, takes as the very foundations of the way 'reasonable human beings' ought to behave, seems to be clearly 'non-sense', or, at the very least, not to be nearly so solemnly right, obvious and valuable as we 'adult' practitioners suppose. It is very difficult to make this point pungently, convincingly and with a proper humility. I can only testify that the more meetings I attend, the more decisions I am privy to and the more discussions I share in, the more I am convinced that most of us most of the time say far less than we think we say, know far less than we claim to know and count for far less than we suppose we do. I do *not* think that this makes us less human, important or valuable. The rest of the book is about *that*. But I am very sure that we cut very different figures from the ones we think we cut. Hence when a group of people with mixed perceptions, motives and understandings in effect say, 'But you're absurd', I am very much inclined to think they are probably right. I am not at all sure that I agree with the particular diagnosis of absurdity or with the remedies proposed or with the tendency, in some quarters, to suggest that remedies are not to be found. How you live with the human condition is a matter for intense wrestling, whether by young or old. The old may well seem immature and foolish. This does not guarantee that the young are immature and wise. But we are, I feel, all a lot more absurd than we generally suppose. And wisdom might have at least a beginning in recognizing this.

Secondly, I think that it is clear that the self-conscious society is capable of very great insensitivities. The actual conditions of life within our societies and of the relationships between them does suggest that all our talk of ideals and values is hypocrisy. The actual goods which our organized, industrial societies are capable of delivering are not very good goods and many of the by-products are monstrous. University life in much of Europe can only be described as lousy. Yet this is the great tradition of enlightenment, of liberal arts, of 'more humane' letters. The professors of these great subjects stand collectively condemned (although I know personally that many of them are humane and liberal men). The tragedy of Vietnam seems to guarantee that no American or any other Western supporter can ever speak credibly again of either democracy or Christianity (not because any American is especially wicked or any Vietcong particularly virtuous). So much liberalism is by proxy. It is not we educated and comparatively wealthy egg-heads who have our jobs threatened, our schools crowded or our houses devalued, for example, by immigrant problems. And so on. Even all this, as with the absurdity mentioned in the first point, can perhaps be lived with, has to be lived with. There may be something to be said *to* the protesters. But I do not see that one can begin to say it if one denies the protesters their right and their need to protest.

Thirdly, I think that Jesus Christ is more likely to be heard if we heed protests than if we ignore them. This is not because I think Jesus Christ is a revolutionary. I have come to the personal conclusion that classifying Jesus Christ as this or that is one constant way in which we try and efface him so that we can go on doing largely what we want to do anyway, with the comfort of claiming the protection of his name. My present conclusion is that Jesus Christ is quite unclassifiable, that he upsets everyone's expectations and that he is far too alive to be pigeon-holed or turned into the latest OK figure. But that is why the attempt to follow him requires our being alert to protests. He cannot be identified with the *status quo*, any more than he can be identified with the latest pattern (of protest or of what you will). He will be concerned with change for the better and with non-acceptance of absurdity, of insensitivity or of good so far achieved which is now being idolized.

Hence it seems to me right and necessary to listen to, and reckon with, the way youth protests to challenge our previous and present ways of asking the question 'What is man?'. We are, in many ways, absurd. We and our societies are in many ways insensitive and Jesus Christ does not lend his name to the unconditional blessing or absolutizing of anything so far achieved or any state of affairs so far existing. But we may surely understand that these very protests provide a most pungent, pointed and poignant way of forcing upon us this question 'What is man?'. We are reminded that it cannot be just a scientific research for more and better organized information. Nor can we be content with any private poetic wrestlings about meaning and satisfaction, experience and event. All this must be in the context of, and in relation to, the living of actual groups of human beings either in society or as outcasts from society. Man may be a reflective self-conscious animal who invents science and dreams up poetry, but he is also a human animal who lives in groups and societies in such a way as to cause himself great misery and contradiction. What he thinks and says about what he does is by no means the same thing as what he is seen to do and be.

So the protest about so much of, at any rate, Western human society does not silence the question 'What is man?'. Rather, it simple strengthens what I have called the 'exclamation' side of this question. What are we to make of, what is there to be made of, being human in all this muddle, protest and confusion?

To proceed with this inquiry, I suggest that we now move back from the considerations of grounds for protest to a sober consideration of the possibilities and powers which seem at present to be, or to be able to be, involved in being a man. The exclamation 'What is man!' may be a cry of pain and despair; we shall have to come back to that. But it may be a cry of excitement and joy. For consider what men have power to do.

2 Exciting Possibilities

Man now knows such a lot that I just do not know how to describe what he knows. This may be bewildering, but it is surely also very exciting. What is man? He is he who knows and who goes on finding out. At this point I want to dwell on the glory of information and know-how and call at least a temporary truce to feelings that poetry might eventually get us further than information in *really* answering our questions and to hunches which suggest that protest is nearer the point than acceptance. Let us consider the poetry of information, and inquire not only what we have to protest about but also what we might have to protest with.

I am afraid of fantasy because I fear both my ignorance and my incompetence, but I can attempt a personal sketch only of how I see man and his knowledge and information situation. It seems to me that man is well on the way to 'breaking the code of the universe' and therefore to having the capacity to make himself by making his environment and to make his environment by the way in which he makes himself. I choose this notion of 'breaking the code of the universe' as a useful central metaphor, suggested in the first place by the extraordinary strides made in understanding the 'genetic code' and, secondly, because it seems to be capable of wide extension to characterize the knowledge situation generally. It is, however, intended as a metaphor and not as a description. Descriptively, 'code' implies encoding by a coder in order to convey information to those who will decode it, possibly with the notion of concealing the information from some others. I am concerned only with the information aspect, and not with any suggestion that the information is 'made available' or is part of any message system involving conscious purposes. I am suggesting that a possible and illuminating answer to the question 'What is man?' is 'the decoder of the universe', but also saying that this is a metaphorical answer. What light, if any, this metaphorical answer might throw on our 'ultimate' understanding of man is for later consideration.

Thus, I use this notion of 'breaking the code' because I see man's extraordinary progress in knowledge about the universe as basically related to analytical success in getting at the basic 'building-blocks' at the various levels of processes in the universe and in understanding how these basic 'units' interact, combine and build up into the complex and dynamic hierarchies and patterns which form the substance of the natural processes on the macro-scale at which we normally encounter them and are part of them. The impression which I get is that it is proving persistently possible to understand large-scale phenomena in terms of small-scale phenomena which can be statistically quantified and related by means of mathematical formulae. So there is happening to every subject dealing with both inorganic and organic matter what happened some time ago to physics, viz.: a macro-subject becomes a micro-subject and the micro-subject advances largely by mathematics. Thus in biology, apart from the development of an immense number of specialisms, we have the development of micro-biology of one sort or another and this goes along with the appearance of biomathematics.

What this means in detail in any one area of study I cannot, of course, understand. One of the significant and problematic things about man's present situation is, surely, that no one can now hope to understand what every one understands. That is to say that it is quite impossible to be an expert on every one's expertise. It would seem that we have, already, more knowledge than we can either know how to know or know what to do with. We shall have to come back to this in the next chapter and subsequently. Meanwhile, I am rashly attempting to give an impression of the overall situation with regard to the whole knowledge-field. Here, what strikes me is the extraordinary success of the analytical method related to more and more refined techniques of investigation at the microscopic level – where 'microcospic' refers to the use of what are, to me, wholly mysterious machines like electron microscopes which make visible structures of an incredible order of smallness.

It is, incidentally, in this matter of dimensions and magnitudes, in the revelation of the almost infinitely small and the vastly great, that I find one of the areas where information and poetry come together or co-exist. I must confess that unless I do some hard and not very congenial thinking, I find it exceedingly difficult to understand people who hold that those discoveries of the micro and macro-dimensions of the universe automatically reduce man to insignificance or somhow empty the universe itself of excitement and mystery. Quite the contrary, as far as I can see. Just as I wish I had more time to read poetry or to listen to music, so I wish I had more time to study such journals as *The Scientific American* or *The New Scientist* where sympathetic attempts are made to convey the feel of developments in research and understanding in so many fields. Whether it be through the work of the poet or the musician or the scientist, it seems that one has the opportunity of confronting something of the quality, of the diversity, of the richness of texture of the universe of which we are parts. It remains remarkable both that the universe is like this and that we can apprehend and appreciate that it is so.

Thus I do not find that man as 'decoder of the universe' is a vulgar, banal or iconoclastic figure. He just continues to be that remarkable thing, a man, disclosing new dimensions of what is remarkable both about him and around him. As he empties the universe of mysteries, so he gets nearer to being able to appreciate, or at least being forced to face, the mystery.

We have, for instance, the 'mysteries' of birth, of the development of life, of the reproduction of the characteristics of the human species in all their complexity and diversity. Thanks to work of great perspicacity and refinement which is still continuing, we are steadily understanding the whole process on both sides, if I may so put it, of the fertilization of a female egg-cell by a male sperm cell. By 'on both sides', I mean that we have an increasingly complete understanding both of how the programming for subsequent development comes to be stored in the respective male and female cells, and of how the process of reproduction and growth develops once the cells have come together.

It is here that we have so striking an example of the phenomenon I point to by the picture-language of 'codes' and of 'building-blocks'. The molecules that contain the genetic information are very complex and the processes they become involved in are, naturally, of multiplying complexity. Nevertheless, it has become possible to describe the exact components of each complexly patterned molecule and the precise nature of the bonds and relationships between the components. It is also becoming possible to give equally accurate descriptions of the processes by which the patterns which are the molecules form interacting patterns with one another, and then build up into higher order patterns which, eventually, are large-scale organisms which develop from human embryos to human beings. In this process of understanding, more and more 'codes' are 'broken'; that is to say, it becomes possible to describe what chemical, molecular or atomic unit comes together in what way and with what, in order to ensure that the necessary information and activity shall be available at the appropriate stage to produce the next form of inter-activity and development. The patterns programme and form themselves, and this programming can be discovered and precisely described.

Just as the initial growth and functioning of human embryos can be understood and described, so can the continuing growth and functioning of the organism from the post-embryo stage to the cessation of growth and function which is death. Nothing like a complete account or understanding is as yet available here, but analogous processes of working out 'codes' and 'building-blocks' seem to be going on in innumerable fields concerned with human physiology and human behaviour. Thus, for example, great strides are being made in the understanding of the brain and the whole nervous system. The sources of particular activities are being located in particular cells of the brain, and it is becoming possible to work out the units of electrical discharge, chemical reactions and the inter-relation between them which constitute the relays between stimuli picked up by this or that part of the body from the external world and the positive response (seeing a red object, moving to keep balance adjusted, etc., etc.) of the whole organism to these stimuli. The point is that it certainly seems as if, throughout the whole range of functioning and behaviour of the human organism, it is possible to correlate the activities and processes of the organism as a whole at the overtly observable level with complex but measurable and comprehensible chains and units of actions and reactions at the micro-level. We are on the verge of being able to describe in precise detail 'what happens' when I see or am angry or feel nausea or perform a sudden jump or whatever it is I do. Moreover, the basic 'building-blocks' of these chains turn out to be things capable of physical measurement (an electrical discharge, a chemical reaction, a node of tissue) and the reactions can be described in terms of physical connections which are capable of observation and quantification.

There is nothing 'mysterious' about all this in the sense of there being happenings which cannot be fitted into the types of observation by which for example neurophysiology or genetic decoding advances. Nor is it necessary to postulate gaps in the physical chains or mysterious encoding entities in the programmes to explain what 'actually' happens or how it 'really' works. The basic units and reactions are simple, physical and quite 'unmysterious', i.e. hide nothing of their nature from refined research and reflection. The apparent 'mysteries' which have puzzled and mystified people and led them to postulate mysterious, magical or supernatural entities at work in a hidden way within the entities of the natural universe have arisen because it is not possible by simple inspection and observation at the gross phenomena level to see or intuit any causal chain between many sets of gross phenomena and many others.

For example, the 'instinct' of animals often produces examples of what look like great mysteries. How do this year's brood of swallows 'know how' to navigate in their first migration from the nesting-site in the north to wintering sites down in Africa, especially when the parents have gone ahead of them? If you study phenomena at the grossly observable level, the level of 'natural history', you can get no further. No 'teaching' procedures can be observed between adults and brood before they split up, no helpful relationships can be observed between flights of flocks and shapes of coastline or other such large-scale features. Is there a mysterious power guiding the swallows or a mysterious gift given to each one of them?

In the sense in which the question is posed the answer is quite clearly 'no'. For instance, we can now make rockets which steer themselves, correct themselves and adjust for unexpected encounters over vast distances with amazing accuracy. We now know about (or some of us do!) mechanisms like feed-back which permit of self-regulative systems. We know how to store information so that it can be activated for use at appropriate moments. We can make machines which choose and so on. We have also discovered a great deal about the processes of evolution and how organisms (not machines) can evolve which have information built into their very genetic make-up. We can see how long processes of selection through adaptation and survival modify and select the information which will be built into the very make-up of the individual members of a species as they are reproduced. Combining these sorts of knowledge and ability (for the evolutionary knowledge may not be capable of direct proof, but the programming of guided missiles is), we have every hope of being able to give an account of migrating swallows which is quite without mysteries (no unsolved puzzles or unknown entities in the chain of description) and which consists entirely in describing units of 'building-blocks' and the 'codings' which relate them.

The example which I have just given seems to me to be particularly useful as we attempt to face up to man's knowledge situation, because it combines reference to machine 'behaviour' and the behaviour of an organism. We have 'guided' missiles and guided birds. Until quite recently we should have had a tendency to use or omit inverted commas as I have just done in the previous two sentences to indicate our discomfort in talking in the same way about non-living things (in this case – missiles) and living organisms (in this case – birds). But one of the major points about this analytical method of research which has made it possible in a multiplicity of ways to 'decode the universe' is that it arrives at physical 'building-blocks' whose relationships and interactions can be described in mathematical terms. At this level of description, processes may apply to machines or to organisms. Hence machine analogies help in understanding organisms and things learnt from organisms can be programmed into machines.

At this point some people are inclined to panic and suppose that we have now proved that the universe is nothing but one vast pre-determined machine or that all organisms, and in particular the human ones, are 'nothing but machines'. In actual practice, the questions of fact, definition and theory which are involved in attempting to sort out the similarities and differences between machines and organisms are quite immense. Anyone who really wants to exercise his mind (whatever may be the proper way of understanding the relationship of mind to brain!) should study discussions about machine intelligence and artificial brains. He will see that simple conclusions are not easily drawn in these fields and that people who are clever at mathematics are not necessarily clever at philosophy and *vice versa*.

But the layman, as most of us inevitably are in these fields, may find this cold comfort. What are we to make of this apparent and worrying erosion of the distinction between something that is a machine and something that is alive? I am suggesting that for the time being we consider it simply as a powerful and positive example of the power which human knowledge has developed to decode the universe. Let us concentrate on the quite remarkable achievements of this method of analysis before we give way to worries about the possible implications of it. Surely the first point for consideration is not that 'mysteries' are being squeezed out of the universe, but that one of the products of the processes of the universe has actually developed the capacity to understand that universe and to do so in a manner which seems to be revealing the secrets of it, in the sense of getting to understand the bits and the ways they go together.

This would not have proved possible unless, alongside the techniques of gaining information about the 'bits' of the universe, men had at the same time been able to develop techniques for handling their information. Thus an essential feature of the present knowledge-situation is the amazing developments in handling and processing information through computers and everything associated with them. Again, to the lay outsider, like myself, there is much difficulty in making a realistic assessment of the situation. Computer-programming languages make great use of combinations of mathematical logic and mathematical notations and conventions which look far more mysterious than they are to persons who have been trained to be literate rather than numerate. Further, the sheer size, in terms of units storing bits of information on the one hand and units capable of producing logical manipulation on the other, produces such numerically vast possibilities of handling and combining information that an effect of bewildering mystery is easily produced. This is the less easily dispelled because of the uncritical enthusiasm with which some practitioners of a still young and incredibly rapidly developing technology press the claims and possibilities of what they are developing.

None the less, and on any account, we do seem to be faced with a sufficiently remarkable example of man's capacity, in one sense, to transcend his own capacities (machines can do things he cannot do) but, in another sense, simply to extend (in hitherto undreamed-of ways) his own capacities (he invents the machines and they work for him). All this comes about, as far as I can see, by a combination of a basically simple analytical approach to information and an increasingly sophisticated range of techniques for storing information and promoting the searching for it, arranging of it and making available of it.

The basic device is that of breaking down our hitherto normal methods of recording information by words (based on letters of the alphabet) or numbers (based on numerals in the decimal system) to one system of enumeration or notation based on what are called the binary digits. Anyone who has advanced at all in mathematics or logic will know all about this, and soon all school children will be familiar with it; for instruction on the basic operations with which computers work are fortunately being introduced in the elementary mathematical education becoming routine in schools. But I am trying to think through this influential feature of the present human situation for myself and for those like me who find ourselves neither as specialized as our contemporaries who work in this field nor as generally literate (or perhaps the word should be 'numerate') as our children in the same field. I shall return later to this developing aspect of our general human situation in which children increasingly take for granted what parents cannot at all, or scarcely, understand. Meanwhile, I must continue with my painstaking attempt to explain in order to evaluate that which I can see to be important, but with which I cannot hope to be either at home or competent.

The point, then, as I see it, of the reduction of notation systems to binary digits is precisely that the digits are binary, viz., that there are only two of them, specifically 0 and 1. Everything then proceeds on a basis of the decimal number 2 instead of the decimal number 10, i.e., 2 (decimal) if written out is 10, 3 is 11 and 4 is 100. 8 is 1000, 16 is 10000 and so on (every power of 2 requires an additional binary digit), while 9 is 1001. All this may seem very clumsy to those of us unfamiliar with it and accustomed to thinking so to speak in 'long hand'. But if one disposes of an electronically operated machine made up of an immense number of 'cells' which can be interconnected and caused to interact with great rapidity, then the situation is very different. Each cell can play its part in storing information by having one of two 'settings' (the equivalent of 0 or 1), or can play its part in furthering calculations or manipulating what information is to be made available by responding to and / or passing on one of two impulses (again, the equivalent of 0 or 1). Of course, elaborate arrangements are necessary for connecting up the 'cells' and the circuits and for programming both the storage arrangements and the impulse arrangements. But the basic possibility lies in being able to 'encode' both information and instructions in terms of the binary digits, which can then be represented or activated by such things as magnetic fields or electrical pulses being given one of two values, directions or forces.

The immense range of possibilities, both by way of calculations and by way of sorting, selecting, arranging and delivering information, arises from the immense number of basically simple operations that can be linked together and gone through at very high speeds. The immense amount of research which has been put into developing computers has enabled the production of smaller and smaller units for storing the bits of information or for registering instructions. This reduction in size has facilitated both the immense speeding up of the reaction time between the various units or through them all, and also the constitution of what, in effect, are bigger and bigger machines in terms of the number of units available (although not in physical size). The size and speed of the processes involved can perhaps be glimpsed by noting some figures reported in the September 1966 number of *The Scientific American* (p. 85), which was especially given over to reporting on information technology. The figures refer to what were then advanced machines, setting the trend for developments in the next few years. A unit is shown which 'provides access in 17 milliseconds to any one of 786,432 36 bit-words or some 4·7 million alphanumeric characters'; i.e., of the coded information stored in that number of 36 bit-groups 'the set you want' can be chosen out and made ready for decoding and delivery to you in ·017 of a second. Another system illustrated 'provides random access in 175 to 600 milliseconds to 800 million bits of information'; i.e., can scan all those units of information for you in something between ·175 and ·6 of a second. No wonder, then, that a scientific calculation which took one of the early *machines* an hour to do in the early 1950s can now be done in a second or so.

Here we have another remarkable example of the way in which man is able to analyse things down to the simplest possible units and to combine this with a highly-developed and developing knowhow about putting things together. I find this power exercised in the development and use of computers analogous to his powers for 'decoding' the universe which I began this chapter by discussing. The basic activities in developing information-processing techniques are not, of course, examples of decoding the universe, but rather of working out ways of encoding and organizing information which has already become available. However, the technical developments in the machines themselves depend on the ability to understand and apply the basic physical processes involved in magnetism, electronics and the behaviour of light and of electricity. Further, the developed machines, and the processes of handling and developing information which become available through them, play a vital part in making possible both the technology which can assist in further exploration of the processes of the universe and in the working out of the results of more and more elaborate experiments. They can help to obtain data and to process data in ways never available before, so that the range of exploration and understanding is immensely widened and deepened. I gain the impression that it is also the case that computers can now assist to suggest the very shape and direction of experiments and in effect 'make suggestions' about lines of investigation in a much more systematic way than mere human reflection on an experimental field would do.

Clearly I am well beyond the limits of my competence to understand or evaluate here, but I have at least got to the threshold of understanding (if not of explaining to anyone else!) why, in some quarters, computers are not only regarded as immensely powerful extensions of the capacities of the human brain but also as well on their way to becoming brains, so to speak, in their own right. Here we are back to a different aspect of the problem referred to at p. 25 above of human beings turning out to be 'nothing but machines'. The point here is that the sophistication of computers seems to have gone well beyond that which is required to programme a missile in such a way that it is 'guided', i.e. able to 'choose' a route, 'select' a target, 'decide' on evasive action, etc. It is comparatively easy to understand how data and instructions could be programmed in to observation and control structures to bring about appropriate reactions to various circumstances and environmental changes. The rub comes when computers can be programmed in such a way that they 'think for themselves' in apparently much more open and unstructured ways than this. The cases where computers assist in suggesting lines of investigation in experimental fields seem to come under this heading. For here, if I understand the situation at all rightly, the computer is not 'deciding' which of a set (however complicated) of previously visualized or programmed alternatives is to be selected in relation to already described goals. Rather, the computer turns out to be able to '*make suggestions*' about lines of action or investigation not previously thought of and, consequently, related to ends not yet visualized.

It is clear that *I* cannot take this discussion any further. But I feel obliged to take it this far because I personally am sufficiently convinced that it is a very real possibility, indeed, I imagine, an already realized possibility, that computers are being developed and programmed in such ways that they behave more and more like brains, including the development of at least some capacity to display what it will be difficult to avoid calling 'originality'. I personally am also the more ready to believe this because I also have the impression that studies of the brain and its links with behaviour likewise suggest that the brain has very many similarities to a computer.

As I also said at p. 25, this is a very difficult field and full of snags for all concerned; but we seem to keep coming back to it. Certainly, I do not see how we can face the question 'What is man?' without facing the apparent possibilities and difficulties here. Perhaps, then, we should face some questions like 'What would be at stake if developments in the design and use of computers, on the one hand, and in the understanding of the operations of the brain, on the other, should decisively show that computers can become brain-like and brains are to be understood as computer-like?'. The chapter I am at present writing is an optimistic one. The pessimistic one comes next, after which we have to see where we can reasonably choose to go. But in the optimistic spirit of this present chapter I want to answer my question somewhat as follows.

What is at stake is our understanding of the possibilities, and therefore responsibilities, of being a man. It is not man's unique existence as man which is at stake, but quite the contrary. It is man's unique existence which is being made clearer and clearer. None of the possibilities that we have glimpsed concerning the uses and the implications of computers give us any necessary reason to go back on the approach which I outlined at p. 26. The remarkable thing is this capacity of man to decode the universe. It is none the less remarkable because the capacity extends to himself. It is true that the fact that man himself comes under the same decoding possibilities as the rest of the universe makes it quite clear that men are homogeneous parts of that universe. That is to say that it becomes clearer and clearer that the 'building-blocks' which make up the human organism and the 'codes' which relate these units are of precisely the same sorts as the units and relations and interactions of the universe, if we press the analysis far enough. Thus we might be inclined to feel that man's uniqueness has been destroyed by this analytical reduction. But such a conclusion is just plain silly (or, as we shall see later, an act of cowardice, perversity, despair or indifference), for who has been able to carry out this analysis? And who has such a brain that he can discover how brains work to the point where it seems likely that he can produce artificial brains? And so on. The answer is quite clear – man. And there is absolutely nothing else like him in this respect. In my view, men (who certainly exist) are far more remarkable than angels (supposing them to exist). For angels are, by definition, pure spirits. There is, therefore, nothing very remarkable or unexpected about their spiritual and intellectual capacities. But men turn out, not by definition but by analysis, to be composed of physically observable units correlated by discernable relationships and interactions. But even so, or perhaps just because of this, they turn out to be capable of spiritual and intellectual activities including the power to decode the make-up both of their environment and of themselves.

It is not, therefore, the uniqueness of man which is in question but the nature and consequences of it. And here we come up against the exciting possibilities which have given the title to this chapter. If you can de-code the make-up of your environment and yourself, then you can re-code them. That is to say that this sort of knowledge provides immense possibilities for control, manipulation and creativity.

The American moon-shots provide excellent symbols, which are also actual examples, of the possibilities here. Men were sent quite beyond their natural environment, in an environment created for them which kept them fully functioning, and then brought back to within a thousand or two yards of a planned spot within seconds of a planned time. The proportionate accuracy on space and time involved here is very high and instances a very high degree of control. It is true that the number of variables involved in the whole operation and the degree of likely variation in these variables are pretty small compared with what is involved in many problems of human society to which we shall soon have to turn our attention. Hence control is very much easier in space flights than in, say, problems of race relations. But none the less, the power for doing really new things which men have is very well symbolized by these successful attempts, even if one can argue a great deal about whether such operations were the right or most presently profitable way of using resources and directing possibilities.

It is clear, at any rate, that real newness is open to man. There are open to him immense possibilities of power and precision. His steadily developing knowledge of the details of all structure and growth must surely encourage him to hope that in the foreseeable future, and perhaps quite soon, cancer will become understood and therefore controllable. As the knowledge of genetics becomes more and more precise, it is surely reasonable to hope that hereditary diseases and distortions can be corrected. There are surely powers available or soon to be discovered which could deal with problems of over-population by a combination of accurate means of birth-control and vast increases in food production. The application of a combination of pharmacological and psychological understanding should enable the control of mental moods and disorders which render so many lives a misery. The combination of communication techniques and teaching techniques should make it possible to bring wide ranges of knowledge and experience within the scope and grasp of everybody. New forms of power should set us free from anxiety about conventional resources which are rapidly being used up. The immensely increased possibilities of planning, prediction and the scanning of vast amounts of individual data at fast rates so that appropriate decisions can very quickly be made ought to allow us to deal with many problems that seem to be getting out of hand in our cities (for example, highly computerized traffic control interconnected over large areas). And all this could go along with a constant pushing forward of the frontiers of knowledge and therefore of what we can do and enjoy. There seems to be very little limit to what man could do and could be set free to do. Liberation from disease, hunger, crowding and depression seems a very real possibility.

But it also seems to many a very remote one, and all the possibilities which I have mentioned, and many others, such as the prolonging of individual lives through improved skill in transplantation and other advances in the medical field, seem to be quite as much fear-inducing threats as exciting possibilities. For while 'man' can do these things (particular members of the human species have discovered how to do them), it does not look as if *men* (human beings in their actual aggregates and groupings) will either allow them to be done or see that they are done properly. Possibilities involve responsibilities and neither societies nor individuals look as if they are organized to enjoy or make a full and creative use of the responsibilities which now arise. While highly systematic work in particular areas has enabled man to emerge as decoder of the universe, the actual effects seem largely random. Man has the power to make himself and his environment in inter-relation and inter-action with one another, but the actual 'making' which is going on is rather a series of fairly haphazard concatenations of events and trends. By-products of human activities pollute the environment. The lives of groups of people are distorted in unexpected, unforeseen or simply unregarded ways by the activities of other groups of people. Thus enthusiastic talk of 'exciting possibilities' can sound extremely like whistling in the dark or drawing rosy prospects out of what is at the best a very uncertain, and at the (quite probable) worst, a very dark future.

But before we go on to face these uncertainties, let us remind ourselves that man as the decoder of the universe including himself is a fact and not a fantasy, whatever fantasies this may seem to threaten us with. The exciting possibilities are there, whatever responsibilities may be discharged or irresponsibilities perpetrated by means of them. In the last chapter I gave my reasons for holding that we ought to pay careful attention to the protest of youth as we tried to weigh up the nature of the question 'What is man?'. As I close this chapter I wish to indicate why I hold that in proceeding further with this question we must take fully into account the understanding of man as the unique possessor of powers of understanding, control and creativity, a decoder faced with the responsibility of consequent encoding or miscoding.

I find that my understanding of the facts of the case and my apprehension of the Christian faith come together very sharply at this point. It seems to me clear that science has established that man is a homogeneous part of the universe, that the basic (i.e., ultimately analysable) rules of his organism are the same as those of the rest of the universe and that he has the capacity to discover this, know this and make use of this. Whatever *else* may need to be said and reckoned with about man, this seems to me to be inescapable. This, however, in no way seems to me to reduce man to a 'non-human' part or parts of the universe. Quite clearly (it seems to me, as a matter of plain observable fact) *within* the universe he 'stands out'. I put 'stands out' in inverted commas because I want to discuss and try and get clear in the last third of the book what this 'standing out' might mean. Further, I do not want to suggest any notion of the 'transcendence' of man until I have to and until I have some chance of indicating what might be meant by it. So 'stands out' is put in inverted commas to indicate that the meaning of the phrase needs further clarification. Man does not literally 'stand out' in the sense, for instance, that he is made of, or partly made of, some non-worldly stuff that would, so to speak, be detectable by super-natural litmus paper but would not cause a reaction to natural detectors. One of the main points is precisely that he 'stands in', i.e., when you analyse to ultimate units and relations there is no difference. But he displays a capacity for the analysis of this very situation in such a way that he can develop an understanding of it and certain controls over it. In this way he both stands out from classification with other organisms (who cannot *invent* anything like themselves – contrast man and his artificial brain-like machines; other organisms can only reproduce themselves), and has power which makes him stand out as an operative and even creative cause in the universe. He is responsible for that of which he can be aware that he is responsible. He therefore *has responsibility* as well as, or instead of, existing as a mere cause. Of course, the responsibility may not make any sense or man may use it or ignore it so as to reduce it to nonsense – we shall consider this in the next chapter. But that there is *something* 'standing out' here within the order of the universe there seems to be little doubt. (We shall also consider in the next chapter why people attempt to explain this away.)

Man, therefore, stands out as the human part, and indeed the human agent, within the universe. This situation is illuminated by and illuminative of three features of the biblical understanding of man and the world which Christians hold to be focused in, and given a definitive direction by, Jesus Christ. The first is the firm presentation of the world as 'created', a belief or approach which is more often encountered in the form that history and its happenings provides the stuff and the occasions in and through which man encounters God, is part of the divine purposes and has a chance to respond to and co-operate with these purposes. It seems to me that the actual position of man and the universe as revealed by science is fully consistent with this understanding and is, as I have said, both illuminated by and illuminative of this understanding. I do *not* think that the scientific position requires the biblical understanding nor that, if we could have really penetrated to the 'logic' of the biblical understanding we should have been able to predict the present scientific understanding. That is to say that I am not attempting to claim or establish any sort of necessary logical connection between a biblical understanding of man's relation to the world at large and a scientific one. It is not my understanding that the insights of faith and the deliverances of science are or can be connected in any such directly logical way. Science is an autonomous activity, and faith (at any rate faith as understood in the biblical and Christian tradition) is to be understood as either a divine gift or a human choice – or, as I would suppose, a combination of both. (For some attempt to explicate this understanding of faith see my introduction, 'The Inquiry of Faith' and postscript, 'The Authority of Faith' in *Living with Questions*, SCM Press, 1969.) But both science and faith (again although I shall not further repeat this, at least faith in the biblical and Christian traditions) are concerned with the same world and the same men. Hence one is concerned with a congruence or convergence, certainly an interaction, between them.

The understanding (by faith) of the world as created and the activities of history as the stuff of the divine-human encounter certainly means that the actualities and realities of the universe and whatever turns out to be the stuff of man's living and exploring in that universe must be taken absolutely seriously as they reveal themselves to be or as they are discovered to be. Conversely, it is, as I say, entirely consistent with this approach to discover that what is involved in being a man, what emerges as the potentialities of man and consequently what is to be seen as the realm of the meaning and ultimate significance of man is all to be discovered in continuity with and in relation to whatever turns out to be the stuff and the processes of the universe. On the biblical understanding of man, man is not different from the rest of the universe in his make-up, nor does the realm in which he has to discover and fulfil his true potentialities lies outside the realm of creation and history. It is true that *God* is conceived of as having his ultimate 'habitation' outside that realm, and we shall return to this. But man's encounter with God and opportunities for discovering his own identity and destiny lie within. It seems to me that the present trends in the scientific understanding of man reinforce and illuminate the need to understand man as a creature who is part of creation, a being in the happenings of history who is produced and required to be both responsive to and responsible for those happenings. Conversely, this biblical faith and understanding illuminates for us the context and depth which we are to give to our understanding of man in his nature as product of the processes of the universe who can yet decode them, and so has possibilities of and responsibilities for the future development and shaping of himself and of his environment.

This illuminating interaction is reinforced by a second feature to be found within the same tradition, namely the claim that man is given dominion by God and is called to co-operate with God, is even to be thought of as in the image of God. Again, there is a mutually enlightening convergence and congruence here. There is no necessary connection which could have been thought of or intuited independently of the way things have actually gone and of the present understanding of the facts of the human situation and potentialities. But as it is, we can now give very concrete examples of man's possibilities of control and dominion within the universe; we see that all the resources of his world *are* delivered into his hands and that he is a creator and shaper of future environments and future identities. In many respects man *is* as God and has the energies of the universe at his disposal. He now seems to be giving actual embodiment to the role which the biblical tradition cast him for, but in only a pictorial and purely imaginative way. It therefore seems to me that my Christian faith forbids me to run away from the notion, in fact the reality, of man as decoder of the universe, of man with all his exciting possibilities of power, control and creativity. Indeed that faith positively orders me to face this situation as something within the purposes of God, i.e., very positively and decisively related to man's ultimate context, meaning, purpose and fulfilment.

Such a confession of faith does not, of course, dispose of all sorts of difficulties which the discussion so far has raised either explicitly or implicitly. In particular, I have done very little to elaborate or justify my statement on p. 22 that 'as (man) empties the universe of mysteries so he gets nearer to being able to appreciate, or at least being forced to face, the mystery'. I believe I have made a step towards this in relating man's ability as decoder to his *responsibilities* as encoder and developer of possibilities. But my attempts to take up the matter much more fully lie in the latter half of the book. All I am arguing at present is that however uncomfortable or unsettling may be the reassessment of man and his situation required of us, any Christian faith we may have does not require us to attempt to deny or distort the emerging facts about men's homogeneity with the universe and powers within it. If men can do these things, then this is a necessary part of any answer we can try and give to the question 'What is man?'. Facts, unfortunately, seem very often to be supposed, both by believers and unbelievers, to be the enemy of faith. If the Christian faith has any valid insights into the way things really are, then this cannot be so. The problem, rather, lies in the experimental and experiential interaction of the bearings of facts and of the understandings of faith. This problem clearly cannot be creatively advanced by faith claiming dominion over facts. But this does not prevent faith from challenging any particular use of facts or allegations about facts. The question here will be whether in facing the question 'What is man?' we find any faith which we can in fact hold as faith and not as fantasy. It is certainly the nature of fantasy to hide from facts.

There is a third aspect of the biblical and Christian tradition and faith which seems to me particularly relevant to whether or not we put great stress on man's power and possibilities in and over the universe in relation to our answering the question 'What is man?'. It is particularly relevant, too, to the question whether my optimistic portrayal of the exciting possibilities open to man is not itself a fantasy, designed consciously or unconsciously to cloud over man's actual situation. This is the understanding that man's exercise of his responsibility in and for the world is always a highly ambiguous thing. (A technical description in terms of the tradition might be that man's exercise of choice is always 'fallen' and 'liable to be sinful', but we shall come back to that later – see Chapter 5.)

Despite the high role for which the Bible casts man ('image of God', 'fellow worker with God', to 'have dominion'), the tradition has no illusions about the way men actually behave. The men of God are very rarely portrayed as godly, the people of God scarcely ever behave as holy and the whole biblical history as it is presented is one long wrestle with the way in which men actually make their responses and exercise their responsibilities. This seems to me to be of fundamental importance as we proceed with our investigation into what is a reasonable assessment of the human situation and see what we can make of the question 'What is man?'. A faith related to the biblical tradition is encouraged to take the highest view of the possibilities and powers offered to man, along with an extremely realistic view of the likelihoods of man's actual behaviour. I do not say a *pessimistic* view, because I am clear that the realism of the biblical view of man, however it has been sometimes interpreted, is basically not pessimistic but optimistic. Again, I return to this in Chapter 5.

The sole point at the moment is that I find my understanding of the Christian biblical faith encourages me in sticking to my estimate of man as decoder and at least partial creator of his universe, not least because this tradition faces up very fully to the possibilities of man's misuse of his powers. We have already had occasion to begin (cf. p. 33) facing up to the factors which turn any 'exciting possibilities' in the minds of many people into threatening possibilities or simply optimistic fantasies. Further, in the first chapter (cf. pp. 14 ff.) we found need to consider the likely validity of the protests of youth against practically the whole of the ordering and thinking of dominant adult society. Man's situation *may* be full of exciting possibilities. It is also very precarious and ambiguous. Yet, at this stage of the argument I still want to maintain a very strong case for taking very seriously the positive side of man's situation and his endowments. For me, the facts of the case (i.e., what science has revealed and what science has enabled or promises to enable man to do) combine with the insights of the Christian faith to encourage this positive evaluation of man's exciting possibilities, not least in the face of the ambiguities of his position. But these ambiguities must certainly be more extensively faced. In the first chapter we saw reason for considering man as a reflective self-conscious animal who invents science and who dreams up poetry, but who also lives in such a way as often to justify pretty fundamental protests about what he actually does and is. We have now explored something more of what is involved in 'animal who invents science' and seen that this can surely be taken as underlining, even as re-defining, man's uniqueness and presenting him as a being with peculiar possibilities and responsibilities. But does this really come to anything much 'in the long run', 'in the end' or 'as far as most people are actually concerned'? For we have to consider what happens to so many of us, what threatens all of us and what we all come to in the end.

3　But it's Absurd !

The picture of man as the decoder of the universe who is thereby enabled to contribute to the construction of his own environment and his own self-development bears little resemblance to life as most human beings experience it. Most of us do not make things happen, they happen to us. Most of us, moreover, do not belong to 'them', that is 'they' who have power over, and control in, affairs. It is other people's decisions which affect us and other people's actions which shape the conditions of our lives. Moreover, the 'exciting possibilities' of the previous chapter do not offer *us* much by way of creativity or control. On the contrary, they look as if they are liable simply to put us at the mercy of another set of 'them' – not the administrators and the politicians this time but the 'experts'. For it is clear that control over and use of the immense developments in communications techniques or the advances in medical and psychological manipulation and care or the planning of individual genetic make-up or group and society population size and so on and so on are all matters which require very specialized know-how, let alone complicated and expensive 'hardware' which ordinary men and women cannot afford, nor could they operate them if they had any access to them.

Hence we have the very real threat of a faceless and remote 'they' reducing the majority, or indeed all, of 'us' to a set of increasingly helpless and statistical-like units. I think that it is here as much as anywhere that the protests of the young members of the affluent societies are particularly relevant to the question 'What is man?'. By trying to develop 'protest' or 'dropping-out' as a way of life, the point is being made that whatever being human means it does *not* mean fitting in to a niche in a vast pattern which is pre-determined or taken for granted for you. It is somehow better, more human, to be your own sort of nonsense than to be somebody else's cipher. Personally, I think that this is absolutely right, a necessary exclamation related to the truth of what it is or might be to be a man and a most important intuition of what is involved or offered in being a human self. The trouble is that the form of the protest so often seems like a protest of sheer despair. The type specimen of this is the protest of that type of drug addiction which leads by way of a series of compulsively necessary 'kicks' to an incurable deterioration and death. The protest on behalf of being human seems to be completely self-defeating.

But this might be precisely the point. The 'exciting possibilities' which have come man's way turn out to be not sources of control and creativity, but rather means of producing destruction and nonsense. The central practical truth about man must be understood to be not that he is the decoder of the universe but that he is the destroyer of himself. There clearly are considerable grounds for such a judgment. The immense developments in computers have received their primary impetus and their largest continuing pressures from the vast missile and space programmes. We learn how to simulate brains in order to be able to deliver the maximum of devastation with the highest possible degree of accuracy and we refine the devices in order to be able to interfere with the enemy's missiles at least long enough for our more sophisticated evasion and then correction techniques to be able to deliver the devastation none the less. It is not merely that the more sophisticated techniques become, the more control seems to fall into the hands of remote experts and of whatever vast governmental or private corporations have sufficient resources to own and run the various machines. It is also that the most notable 'positive' uses of the new powers and possibilities seem so far to have gone in actual (cf. Hiroshima) or possible (cf. the missiles) negative and destructive directions.

Further, there is not only the threat of a remote 'they' who will steadily reduce 'us' to anonymous ciphers if they do not actually blow us up or kill us off by radiation by-products. It is very questionable whether there exists anywhere a 'they' who are really in control in any overall way at all. Here, I think, everyone, whether the so-called 'powerful', or the evidently 'powerless', becomes 'we' i.e., just men bound up in one common situation. This is, basically, a situation of change which is so rapid that we cannot adjust to or adapt with it fast enough to exercise affective control over it. There are so many sources of innovation motivated in so many different ways and interacting with one another in such a variety of uncontrolled or unforeseen fashions that the overall effect is one of randomness from the strictly human point of view, i.e., the trends which emerge are not (very often) foreseen and certainly not chosen, but just happen as far as any politicians, legislators or directors are concerned. Men are in the position, collectively, of having to react to a vast and growing network of effects, trends and changes in their environment which were originally initiated by particular groups or activities but which have combined together to produce something under no one's control and with its own momentum, or, rather, momenta.

Men have, in fact, produced such a *turbulence* in their overall environment that it is very questionable whether control can be gained over the various trends in it; yet it seems quite possible that unless various situations are controlled, the environment will cease to be suitable to support and promote human life. A further complication is that the nature of the controls which need to be introduced seem, in at least some very important cases, to be in conflict with what have hitherto been taken to be important human values.

One aspect of this turbulence is the knowledge-explosion to which reference was made in the last chapter. One cannot control what one does not know about. But, as I said, no one can know what everybody knows; i.e., the sum total of all the specialisms of knowledge is quite beyond the grasp of any one man or group of men. Nor does there seem to be time, even if there were the means and the will, to take special dispositions to cope with this situation, such as by setting up highly skilled inter-disciplinary groups of persons who might, with the aid of elaborate computers and a large staff, succeed in getting some over-view of the situation. The time factor is very important here because knowledge and research is breeding knowledge and research and this has the general effect of specialisms of knowledge flying further and further apart from their common centre at an ever increasing speed. The situation will not stop for us to catch up with it, even if we (i.e., those in a position to do so) were willing and ready to do something about it.

Moreover, consider the likely situation if there were groups of such computer-equipped 'know-alls'. Who could be trusted with such power? Man as the decoder of the universe seems to have produced an insoluble puzzle for himself. Any solution looks as if it is practically moving out of his reach at an accelerating pace. Further, it also seems likely that if any solution were attainable it would be at least as threatening to our humanity as is living with the puzzle – even though 'the puzzle' may resolve itself by blowing up completely.

A particular problem within the whole field of the knowledge-explosion is the effect whereby more and more people live in a world which is completely strange to the generation or generations before them and also to whole societies of people who live still in less developed parts of the world. Literally, it is the same world and this, so to speak, more than ever before. The diffusing and cushioning effects of time and space are now almost entirely cut out by modern methods of communication. (Television and air-travel are two very notable examples, especially the former, of the way everyone is liable to be affected by what might be called instantaneity and ubiquity. You do not have months or years gradually to absorb immensely diffused shock waves emanating from centres of disturbance in cultures or countries quite different from your own. Some impact of such things arrives among you practically as soon as it happens.) Thus the world is not only one world as a physical entity in the universe, it is much more psychologically and experimentally one world than ever before. The description of the world as a 'global village' is, in some ways, literally apt. For example, a rumour, fashion, or protest started in some developed northern country can get talked about in some less developed southern one in next to no time, just as in rural villages what the village postmistress knew used to reach the vicarage kitchen with uncanny speed. But in another sense, classes and groups of people who are living in this same one world are psychologically and experientially worlds apart.

This is the case with people who live literally next to one another, indeed, in the same family. The fierceness or sharpness of the generation gap is an example of this. The 'wisdom of the elders' looks pretty silly in a world which takes guided missiles, the possibility of nuclear explosion, TV, electronics, immense social mobility and computer-type operations for granted. But the elders cannot possibly do this 'taking for granted' or get very far in comprehension because this is not the world in which they grew up and inherited the wisdom of *their* elders. But what *is* the wisdom for a world with an accelerating knowledge explosion, an increasing generation gap and an increasing degree of change and turbulence which cannot fail to affect everybody?

There seems to be a very strong likelihood that just as the decoding of the universe threatens to be self-defeating by producing even more insoluble puzzles (puzzles, too, which have a dynamic of their own which is far more threatening than 'undisturbed' nature seems to have produced), so the beginning of the experiencing of the world as truly one world, a global village, bids fair to make it more and more difficult for men actually to live together with any degree of understanding or harmony. The turbulence extends to very intimate and basic relationships. Man, then, is not only, self-reflectively, a great problem to himself, he is also, objectively, a great producer of problems for himself. And these problems are threatening at every level of his existence.

A particular problem which could threaten the continuing existence of the human race in the not very distant future and which is also a powerful example of the way in which man contributes to causing changes in his environment which he neither consciously initiates nor seems able to control, is that of population growth. At the present time the rate of population increase over the whole world averages out at between 2 and 3 per cent per year. That rate would produce over a *doubling* of world population by the end of the century. (Estimated population in 1965 of 3,300 millions; projected by many experts in 2000, population of 6,900 to 7,000 millions.) There is now much argument as to whether a number of trends, in particular the development and promotion of simpler and simpler effective birth control techniques, will substantially slow up this trend. But on any showing there is something of a 'biological time-bomb' getting nearer and nearer to explosion here. How are all these people to be fed at any reasonable level? A vast percentage of the world's population is not fed at such a level now. Yet improved techniques related to elementary health and sanitation, famine relief and various other palliative measures even when spread so thin that they *only just* keep people alive, none the less do keep them alive in vast numbers.

The overall problem of gross population increase of course conceals a multitude of different problems within it. For example, a rising birth-rate contributing to the increase is unevenly distributed.

On the whole, it is developing countries which 'suffer' from it, so that such countries may well find that it takes all their economic efforts to keep a rapidly rising population at just about the same low standard of living. This is one of the reasons why the poor may well get poorer while the rich get richer. In affluent countries the old tend to live longer and longer. How are they to be supported and what are they to do with themselves as they have longer and longer life-spans that are not occupied in the 'productive' side of the lives of their society? Very strong pressures are building up which suggest that both the reproduction and the prolongation of human life needs controlling, at least if we look at the overall picture. Compulsory birth control almost seems a necessity and some form of euthanasia at least something desirable – otherwise what *quality* of life can we expect in an overcrowded globe? But what quality of life would it be for individuals under such organized compulsions? Are they better or worse than unorganized compulsions, like hunger or crowding into cities which become more and more unmanageable, as Calcutta already seems to have become and as New York threatens to become?

It begins to look as if man has somehow and by his own bootstraps, so to speak, pulled himself out of the ecological niche in which he evolved but that he is not collectively capable of doing what is necessary to keep things sufficiently under control to construct the new ecology and environment which would permit him any sort of stable and expanding existence. Perhaps he is not so very different from the lemmings after all, and no freer from the impersonal and indifferent balances and checks of nature than they are. A certain sequence of events, for which, of course, the lemmings have no responsibility and of which they have no reflective awareness, causes a situation so 'favourable' to their development that they reach a point of overcrowding at which a migration is set in motion which leads them to mass suicide. And the 'balance of nature' is restored. How near are we to such a 'swarming' of men – perhaps in the form of wars precipitated by the desperate pressures of hungry have-nots against over-fed haves? The decoder of the universe is certainly very far from being the controller and systematic developer of his environment and societies.

So far I have been trying to point to the control/need for control/ lack of control situation. There seems a good case for concluding that individuals or groups of men may be very powerful in particular ways, but that collectively man remains pretty helpless. But if we turn from trying to think about the cumulative effect of mass phenomena and trends to consider the actual ways in which men tend to exercise power where they have it, or think they have it, then the situation could be thought to be even worse. For here we are confronted, not merely with lack of control or foresight or capacity to take needful decisions, but with repeated examples of what can surely only be called mis-control. The diagnosis (and indeed the prognosis) for sin may be a matter for endless dispute, but its existence seems an obvious fact: men again and again display a flawed way of acting, a capacity for a total disregard of other men as men, a pleasure in the practice of cruelty, a capacity for self-deception, and a restrictive pettiness and pomposity of personal power which constantly frustrates hopes of vast and peaceful sharings of increases in human welfare. Moreover, such aspects of human behaviour can easily become the focusing cause of appallingly deep inflictions of misery and suffering which can expand to a vast scale.

It is difficult to dwell imaginatively, coolly and hopefully on what man have actually done and do actually do to other men, and not least on what not particularly 'bad' men do, cause to be done or allow to be done. The amount of human misery is very great. And in any case, the actuality of one tortured, neglected and dying child is more than can be borne, if you actually reflect about it. Further, whatever may be said about natural disasters, disease and so on, a very large part of the immense weight of all this misery is humanly caused or humanly aggravated. I have claimed in the previous chapter that man is clearly a unique animal in his capacity for understanding himself and the universe and therefore for standing out in the universe and among animals. This must be balanced by what seems the equally clear fact that man stands out among the animals by his capacity to be bestial.

Indeed, the very use of this adjective 'bestial' of human conduct is probably a powerful example of the way in which men conceal aspects of their own reality from themselves. For it is not a quality of 'brute beasts' to be 'bestial' in the sense in which that adjective is generally used. Deliberate cruelty, sustained aggressiveness carried through to the deliberate destruction of fellow members of

46

one's species, either by destruction of livelihood, or of character or by actual death and many other forms of 'brutal' treatment by men of one another, are not to be paralleled among the other animals. 'Nature red in tooth and claw' is largely a human myth and a human projection on to the jungle of that which is much more characteristic of the city or of other human settlements.

Now, just as we considered in the previous chapter certain very positive aspects of man's ability to understand, control and create within the universe, so we shall later consider certain very positive aspects of man's dealings with man, of behaviour by the human animal which stands out in what we should much more willingly recognize as a human rather than a bestial way. But in our attempt to make some sort of realistic survey of what is actually involved in the human situation we do clearly have to take very full account of the fact that very negative aspects are mingled with very positive ones. On the aspect of man as decoder of the universe and creator of himself and of his environment versus man as disturber and distorter of the earth and destroyer of himself and polluter of his environment I just do not know where the weight of the evidence ought finally to be judged to lie. I think that if I compel myself to face up to the impression which what I might call the 'unvarnished' evidence has made upon me, then I must admit that this evidence tends to come down on the pessimistic side. That is to say, that it looks as if the trends of uncontrolled changes developing towards uncontrollable changes, of turbulence increasingly leading to more and more instability, of men creating more and more problems for themselves with which they find it increasingly impossible to deal or even live, are the trends which are most likely to prevail. The situation seems far nearer to being out of control than to being under control.

That, I say, is my impression of the 'unvarnished' evidence. By 'unvarnished' I mean the evidence taken as far as possible in its own right and on the assumption that it is this sort of evidence alone which is really relevant for making predictions about man's future situation and for making deductions about the way man and his possibilities are to be assessed. Of course, strictly speaking, there is no 'unvarnished' evidence; i.e., no evidence, of this sort especially, is collected 'neat' and without presuppositions. Further, not even experts (on futurology and the like, i.e., the surveying, correlating and extrapolating of trends in the world situation under various aspects) can be very accurate about the evidence, and I am certainly not one of such experts. And, finally, no assessment of such (very partial) evidence can be made without further presuppositions. This makes the whole exercise extremely precarious. None the less, I do not think that this gives one a comfortable excuse for hoping vaguely that all will be well. Evidence in the form of likely projections of populations, likely distribution of wealth, lists of likely inventions and of the effects of these and of others already made, reports on the effects of urbanization and of consequent problems, facts about pollution and about the using up of resources and so on, all these things, taken in as 'unvarnished' a way as possible seem to encourage pessimism rather than optimism. The problems man is creating for himself seem to delineate man as more of a problem-maker than a problem-solver and it looks as if the problems could easily become ones of life and death, with the probability on death.

The case for this way of interpreting things, apart as I say from any 'varnish' which it might seem proper to apply because of some deeper, broader and more widely hopeful insight which it is claimed should be adopted, seems to be strengthened by the impression made by what might be called the natural and general history of man's ways of dealing with man. There *is* much that is human in man's dealing with man and to this, as I say, we shall be coming. But there is so much that is appalling. I see no point in going in for any catalogue of 'man's inhumanity to man'. Justice to it can only begin to be done by the novelist, the poet, the painter (cf. Picasso's *Guernica*) or the historian when he is permitted to perform as an artist. The reality, moreover, is intolerable. And prose sermons on the subject are simply tedious catalogues of moralizing which allow the discharge of moral indignation in such a way as to prevent all involved from facing up to sharing in the monstrous immorality or the baffling amorality of the whole thing. What men do to men is insufferable, and it is terrible that the sufferers have no escape from this suffering.

It is difficult, therefore, to be easily assured that there are factual grounds, especially related to a likely view of future prospects, for a positive and optimistic answer to the question 'What is man?'. For all his self-reflection and his poetry, his protests, his scientific ability and his power to decode his universe and himself, he seems to deal very badly with himself and to be rather more likely to be his own executioner than his own fulfilment. The exciting possibilities seem to have every chance of leading to absurdities and the notion of man as responsive to and responsible for his own possibilities and his own environment seems to be, on balance, not hopeful sense but threatening nonsense.

There is a type of writing and arguing about man and his nature enjoying a certain vogue at present which combines the emergence of man as a decoder of his own nature with reflections on man's lack of responsibility in dealing with his fellows in an interesting and possibly significant manner. This line of approach is reflected in various ways in such books as *The Territorial Imperative* by Robert Ardrey; *On Aggression* by Konrad Lorenz; and *The Naked Ape* by Desmond Morris. The general method is to draw the 'building-blocks' or units with which man's nature is to be decoded from evolutionary theory and from the study of animal ecology and behaviour, that is to say, from the study of the way animals interrelate with their environment and of the way in which this is related to the formation and adaptation of their patterns of behaviour.

The results which are drawn from this method purport to show that the present pattern of man's behaviour towards his fellows is to be understood and explained in terms of where the unit-blocks of animal behaviour patterns have evolved and adapted to in his case. Man, for various reasons, has not evolved ritualized (and therefore harmless) ways of dealing with intra-specific aggression (i.e., attacks between members of the same species) as have, for example, geese and wolves. The territorial imperative is a general feature of animal life (protection of 'space' in which to live, obtaining a defence of a 'home', etc.); at an early stage in his evolution man's aggressiveness took a particularly sharp and carnivorous turn; we are therefore bound to produce a perpetual pattern of inter-group struggles, individual conflicts and, quite possibly, wars. The way to understand our behaviour is in terms of our ape-like ancestry (itself understood in terms of the way it is alleged archaeology shows 'apes' to have behaved) and the way apes are now alleged to behave and the modifications consequent upon our having evolved in the direction of nakedness. From this we can be clear what to

49

expect within *The Human Zoo*, as the second of Dr Morris's books is entitled.

Two things are significant here. First, the use of the method, already referred to, of constructing your patterns of understanding, explanation and prediction from 'building-blocks' which are put forward as scientifically determined by methods of observation and analysis similar (in their respective fields) to the methods I discussed in the previous chapter. Thus we appear to have an application to patterns of human social behaviour of the decoding methods which have been so successful elsewhere. Secondly, the method as used provides an explanation of these patterns which shows that 'you cannot expect anything else'. This means that there are no grounds for feeling surprised or distressed, still less guilty, about the way in which man's irresponsible behaviour towards man threatens to make nonsense of any notion of his 'responsibility'. The writers themselves seem to have varying degrees of moral purpose and moral urgency in their own approaches. All desire that we should face our situation as realistically as possible and would, presumably, see this as the responsible and truly human attitude. Lorenz is so concerned with the urgent need to deal with aggression that he writes more and more as a propagandist and sounds like a moralist. Hence there are no grounds for questioning the moral purposes of the writers as individuals. And, in any case, if they had got their facts right and their deductions reasonable, moral imputations would play their too-frequently immoral role of being used to undermine unpalatable but irrefutable evidence on irrelevant grounds.

But what is interesting is that they have almost certainly got both their facts and their deductions wrong, and also that their line of argument has been received with such enthusiasm, to judge by the sale of the books, discussion in the press and on TV, etc. Whatever else man is, he is neither naked nor an ape. The fallacies in analogizing from (in any case captive) geese to human behaviour are easily exposed (and much of Lorenz's 'field evidence' in a variety of cases is simply countered by quantities of contrary evidence by other experts). Ardrey's selection of his evidence can be shown to be tendentious even where it is actually evidence. The documentation for this can be most simply obtained through two small publications, *Naked Ape or Homo Sapiens?* by Bernard Towers and John

Lewis, and *Man and Aggression*, edited by Montagu Ashley. The tone of some of the counter-contributions, especially in the latter collection, indicate that we are in fact in the middle of a propaganda battle about how we should reasonably regard man, so all the distortion is probably not on one side. None the less, it does seem pretty decisively established that none of the books in question will stand up as valid uses of the scientific decoding method, whatever interesting (and accurate) information they may provide at particular points.

We are left, therefore, with the importance of the books as significant and popular examples of the thesis that 'Science shows that man is nothing but an animal' and that, therefore, we are in no sense to be blamed for the way in which we fail to handle the more objectionable features of our animal nature. We are simply living up to it. At p. 31 I expressed my view that to draw from the discovery that man was made up of the same building-blocks as the rest of the universe the conclusion that his uniqueness was thereby destroyed was 'just plain silly' or an act of 'cowardice, perversity, despair or indifference'. After we have been confronting, not the successes of man as decoder of the universe, but the actual and likely failures of man to live in a humane way or to control the effects of his power to human promoting ends, this may seem to be somewhat of a harsh judgment. Reductionism (man is nothing but an animal and must be expected to behave accordingly—we must take what precautions, if any, that we can) might seem to be the reasonable man's refuge and about the only comfort open to us. At least we are not to blame for what we may have to suffer or may inflict. There is no need to add cosmic guilt to physical discomfort. But the trouble is that the 'nothing but animals' line as worked out by Lorenz and the others is not descriptively accurate. Man cannot by these means be reduced to a non-human animal (say, a naked ape). He remains, descriptively, very much a human one. He may not be able to make sense of, or humanly discharge, his human possibilities of response and responsibility, but a descriptive discharge of them by explaining them away does not lie this way, at any rate. It looks as if 'the mystery of absurdity' is not easily got rid of. Man remains burdened with being human. His situation is not that of being an unnecessarily neurotic animal. He remains an absurd man, for he retains his capacities to reflect, to stand out, to pursue aims, to consider values, to love, to care and to be troubled by his failures in all these respects.

So far, then, man's uniqueness cannot be dissolved away, either by means of insisting on the homogeneity of his basic units of composition with the rest of the universe or by attempts to reduce him from the status of a *human* animal. But there seem very strong grounds for inclining to the view that his uniqueness 'does him no good'. Hence is it silly, cowardly, perverse or anything other than a reasonable act of despair or indifference to make use of some escape route or other from any positive evaluation of this uniqueness? At any rate, the fact that something cannot be explained away does not thereby imply that sense can be made of it. What do you do when you cannot make anything satisfactory of uniqueness or satisfactorily make away with it?

I should say that this is the situation we have to face, this is what has to be taken into account in answering our question 'What is man?'. For instance, one might attempt the provisional formulation 'man is, or tends to be, a contradiction to himself and a contradiction of himself', and then see if there is any possibility of going on from there. What is the objection to facing a tension, even if it looks capable of building up into a contradiction, if the evidence for both sides of the tension, or for both strands which threaten to produce the contradiction, seems to be strong? It may well be that with the formulations set out in this paragraph we have reached the stage in an argument or an exploration at which choices made without explicit and far-reaching pre-suppositions are quite impossible. We have perhaps come to a point where we have to choose with what sorts of exclamations we respond to the information available to us. This would mean that we are now confronted with an aspect of our discussion which I tried to bring out in the first chapter when I suggested that in answering the question 'What is man?', information might not prove to be enough and that, indeed, the question would prove to be as much an act of exclaiming as a process of asking, as much a deciding on reactions as an assessing of information.

Those who make use of approaches to the problem of man along the lines of 'man is nothing but a naked ape' or 'man is basically an aggressor' have opted for a pessimistic reaction to the human situation and have selected information accordingly. Indeed, the reactions of other experts in the field seems to suggest that they have even distorted information accordingly. It looks as if this arranging of evidence to give a 'natural account' which justifies a pessimistic view of man is at least to some extent designed consciously or unconsciously, to relieve men of any burden of anxiety about any sharing of their own in that behaviour which contributes to the pessimistic view of man. Certainly the line of argument can be taken in that sense. It is this aspect of the matter which warrants the introduction of terms like 'cowardly' or 'perverse'. It is certainly dangerous to introduce terms of this nature, and may seem to presage a slanging match in which emotion is substituted for evidence. But I do not think that the danger can be avoided, because we shall not do justice to the real nature of the question 'What is man?' if we do not explicitly allow reactions and emotions to be part of the evidence.

Men who encourage other men to believe that they are fitted 'by nature' only to be members of a 'human zoo' must be prepared to face the charge of cowardice on the grounds that they are preparing for themselves and urging on others a speciously justified way of avoiding having to face what is involved in being a man. Men who choose to emphasize the aggressive, unlovely and unloving qualities of men as being *the* characteristics of their ancestors and therefore of themselves must face the charge of perversity on the grounds that they are choosing to promote as decisive what, on their own showing, are the less attractive and, if there were any choice in the matter, less desirable sides of what is involved in being human. Such attitudes, then, can reasonably be held to be expressions of despair or indifference. Either the overall human situation is despaired of so that release has to be found by giving an account of it which mitigates the despair into natural history (otherwise why choose to spin this fabric of evidence and explanation?) or else there is indifference to the full range of possibilities in the human situation (or why ignore the other side of the picture?). You do not evade the responsibilities of being a man by selectively explaining why man cannot be held responsible. You simply discharge your own human responsibility in a particular way. A way, moreover, which, I would suggest, deserves to be called a bad and inhuman one. It is surely an abuse of science to conceal reactions and choices which plump for the pessimistic and irresponsible side of things under the guise of scientific accounts or popular accounts of 'what science has shown'.

However, there are better reasons for being pessimistic about man than ones provided by pseudo-evolution or pseudo-ecology. We were considering some of them in the earlier part of this chapter, and the work of such as Morris and Ardrey, together with the general reaction to it, could be held to strengthen these reasons. Man can be seen as constantly failing to measure up to, and again and again making harmful uses of, the possibilities and powers that come his way. He seems to prefer his degradation, to choose for instance to consider himself rather as a naked ape than as a responsible human being. Perhaps, therefore, there is no positive way of facing the situation which I formulated tentatively (on p. 52) as 'man is, or tends to be, a contradiction to himself and a contradiction of himself'. Even if we can avoid what I have called the cowardice of failing to face the full extent of the human dilemma or the perversity of chosing the inhuman side of the evidence about human beings before we are compelled to, yet we may still find that our 'courage' and 'good sense' are still empty gestures. For what are we to make of this very ambiguous history and state of man, in which he does so many inhuman things and which leads him sometimes to attempt to dissolve the contradiction by denying that he is *uniquely* 'man' at all and is to be considered fully and simply along with the rest of the animals?

4   Well, is it ?

I should like to draw attention (briefly and therefore more than usually inadequately) to three influential attempts to deal with this contradiction of man, attempts which have contributed, and do contribute, to the way men think and judge about themselves, before I go on to try and explain what I make of the distinctively Christian attempt.

The first is that associated with the name of Freud. I should say that its influence as a dominating mythology of explanation is very much on the wane, although the thinking of Freud and that inspired by him has left a pervasive influence, diffused in various ways, through man's thinking about man. Here man's sense of contradiction is understood entirely as something internalized. The dynamics of the psychic development of every child, from the internal experiences in the womb, through the first relationships to and reactions with the mother to all the pattern of extending relationships and reactions in upbringing, produce an internal pattern of psychical life, which has a dynamics of its own. This dynamic works largely at the unconscious level and consists of a series of checks and balances, repressions and drives which can be balanced or unbalanced in an immense variety of ways but which is, in any case, a system of stresses and conflicts. To be 'adjusted' is to have the conflicts sufficiently in balance to be able to live a 'normal' life in 'normal' society (whose own stresses and strains, incidentally, produce the 'abnormalities'). To be 'maladjusted' is to have some aspect of some conflict so over-developed that the whole psychic life is distorted and normal sharing in normal life becomes impossible. Psychoanalysis by skilled and sensitive practitioners may bring sufficient of the components of, and contributions to, such a conflict sufficiently into the conscious awareness for the acute stress to be taken out of them so that some sort of psychic balance is restored and a comparatively normal life becomes again possible. But, in any case, all life is conflict and the 'good' life is conflict sufficiently balanced to avoid overt and crippling stress. To find yourself a 'contradiction' from time to time is simply to become aware of an imbalance in your psychic life which is so constructed by its own dynamics as to be some resultant of contradictory forces in any case.

Freud did make some attempts to use his theories, which were basically the result of reflection on and systematization of sensitive clinical observation and practice in relation to mentally disturbed persons, to give an overall account of man's psychic development from primitive man onwards. But the results are so obviously sketches of mythological scenarios that no one could now mistake them for providing a descriptive causal chain of the 'building-blocks' which constitute the basic units of human development and behaviour and of the type which scientific rigour requires. What is still not always clearly or readily recognized is that his account of the internal dynamics of the psychical life of the individual is not a scientific one either. For example, the 'ego', 'super-ego' and 'id' are not in the least like DNA molecules, nor are the relationships between them or the experiences or reactions which are said to go into the 'building-up' of them in the least like chemical reactions, electrical discharges, or power centres. Freud's 'units' are *wholly* conceptual ways of producing *mental* diagrams which serve to explain and convey the construction he has made out of his intuitive experience and practical 'successes'. There is nothing about them which is analysable or measurable by the methods and machines appropriate to scientific units and relations. Hence neither Freud nor his followers and developers in any way provide us with a scientific account of human psychological make-up. This is not to say anything directly about the usefulness or uselessness of Freudian practice. Practical arts gained from sensitive observation and experiment may well convey their 'know-how' through a mythology which is experimentally based and experimentally applied. But it does mean that Freud and 'Freudianism' (in any form which may still exist) are not sources of straightforward information about the make-up of man which we are bound to accept in the form offered for forming our own judgment about this make-up in relation to answering the question 'What is man?'.

If we *choose* to take a Freudian approach as determinative of our whole understanding of man (and this would be a matter of choice and certainly not of 'scientific necessity' – whatever that might mean), then we shall, presumably, adopt a very sceptical view on the subject of human responsibility and a very pessimistic view of human life as a whole. For as a 'total' account of what is involved in being human Freud presents men as, at the best, making the best of a bad job, i.e., arriving at the least troubling balance of conflicts that is practically possible, in the midst of 'civilization and its discontents'. However, the status of Freud's approach does not compel us to choose him and pessimism, although pessimism might incline us to choose his approach.

He has, however, had a 'revelatory' effect on our approach to, and understanding of, human behaviour. We are now warned, surely decisively and permanently, that human motivation and human capacity to comprehend are hardly ever, quite possibly never, what they seem. Our conscious and self-conscious actions and reactions are certainly only part of us, not necessarily, at any given moment, the determining part of us. Freud has certainly provided some more very powerful evidence, whatever its precise status, of man's ambiguity. He has warned us to mistrust any spontaneous or immediate diagnosis we might make of ourselves or of others. We have to allow not only for *subjectivity* but for the fact that our subjectivity, our reactions and our judgments about our reactions, is shaped by that which is not known to us and of which we may not be aware. Thus we have one more apparent difficulty in the way of easily accepting our picture of man as the decoder of the universe who can understand and control his environment and himself. For Freud has at least raised very searching questions about the trustworthiness of the way in which we react to what we know or think we know. Also, even if he does not provide us with a necessary and acceptable explanation of our experiencing ourselves as contradictory, he has certainly powerfully underlined that that is a very common feature of the human condition. We are left, then, with further evidence of the confusion of this human situation and with questions about the possibility of human freedom and about the validity of human judgments to which we shall have to return in a later chapter. Perhaps, after all, insights into the limitations on our freedom of choice and on our accuracy of judgment may help us to greater freedom and accuracy.

Or perhaps they may simply make clearer the illusory nature of all that we have held to be most important about us. Even so, I think I should still be impressed by an illusion that knew itself to be an illusion. There would be, in this very experience, some ground for supposing that what was involved in the illusion was an important reality.

But the question would still remain about what sort of reality and why the illusions and contradictions. Karl Marx has been the source of what has now become a living tradition of continuing thought and action with a highly influential approach and answer to these questions. In a way, Marx's basic answer has a shape very like that of Freud's but turned inside out. For Freud, man's contradictions and illusions are internalized, produced by his individual psychical development. For Marx, man's contradictions and illusions are externalized, produced by the social and, especially, economic development of his environment and his relationships. The contradictions which man experiences and which he embodies are part of the dialectic of history which itself evolves by the conflicts of opposites (thesis and antithesis) producing resolutions (synthesis) which form stages in the evolutionary process and the basis of the next set of conflicts. This is to be very concretely understood and related to the particular stage of the process one is part of. In this way man can become an active participant in and promoter of the conflict to the ultimate point where the contradictions will be overcome in a synthesis which allows full participation and fulfilment by all involved without conflict and contradiction. Meanwhile a positive meaning and purpose can be found in the conflicts.

This (essentially Hegelian) dialectic is related to history and the particular situation of particular societies and classes within societies by an understanding of social and economic interaction which, it is alleged, is an accurate scientific description of what has happened, does happen and will happen. Basically, the set-up is such that man is alienated from himself by being alienated from the control of his own labour and the fruits of it. There is always a ruling and exploiting class and a ruled, exploited and deprived one. This distorts all men, for the exploiting class are distorted in their understanding, actions and reactions by the need to defend and maintain an exploitive order of society. (At the present stage of history, capitalism.) The exploited are distorted by the sufferings of their exploitation and deprivation. Thus the interests of the exploiting ruling class and the exploited working class are themselves in conflict, the product of a contradiction, and the producer of contradictions. The resolution lies in working for the revolution of the exploited class or classes to establish the proletariat as the ruling class under which a society can be developed which is not based on exploitation and conflict but which moves towards the classless society to which each can contribute according to his ability and from which each can receive according to his needs. Thus man's alienation and contradiction are taken as the essential clue to what is going on in history and to the possibilities in the nature of man. They are, moreover, clues which permit of a positive approach to the negativities of history and the human situation. The exploiting classes have, one way or another, to be liquidated, but man, embodied in the exploited and deprived, has a very positive future.

The case of and for Marxism can be put with great force and a wealth of philosophical insight and analytical detail of a political, social and economic nature. Moreover, the whole tradition has now generated and does continue to generate its own discussions, insights and discoveries. On any account we have here something which has had an immense impact on political history, social thinking and human living and which continues to be one of the main sources, in practice, of both insight and activity in the world. Any continuing investigation of the question 'What is man?' must be seeking some sort of conversation (containing, inevitably, negative and positive elements) with the various strands of this tradition and practice. None the less, I cannot see that its basic tenets are believable or acceptable on their own terms.

Marxism cannot establish any claim to be scientifically based, in any strict sense. The various forms and versions of Marxism (for whatever claims may be maintained in some quarters, there is now clearly no decisively canonical version of the true faith) are clearly various forms of an ideological over-view rather than variations of descriptions of a strictly scientific nature, which are limited in their scope to what the evidence can be reasonably held to necessarily support. The all-embracing claims made by Marxism for explaining the whole nature of reality (i.e., for defining the context of under-standing within which one must interpret what one discovers about reality) surely establish beyond a doubt that its basis is not scientific.

(This is *not* necessarily the same thing as to establish that it is false.) For scientific evidence is not the sort of evidence which, of itself, establishes any over-view. Scientific evidence describes what it describes and cannot go any further. Men may then choose to interpret this evidence as either leading them to, or fitting in with, overall views of the whole and ultimate nature of reality, but while this is a humanly human activity it is not a scientifically human activity. We shall have to return to this human habit of using scientific or other information and observations for making cosmic exclamations which look like explanations (query – a possible answer to the question 'What is man?' – a reflective animal who is not sufficiently adjusted to his own reflective capacities so that he has to hide from the fragmentary and absurd nature of the universe behind unifying fantasies he has constructed for himself?). We have here a question which is broader than that of Marxism, but meanwhile I think it is sufficient to raise it, to dispose of Marxism's claims to draw its authority from science, even if it is alleged to rest on a scientific approach to the social and economic sciences.

It is, in any case, very doubtful how far the last-named 'sciences' can lay claim to the rigours of scientific method in their practice and therefore to the assuredness of scientific results in their conclusions. But even this does not have to be pursued, as observers, historians and analysts of political, economic and social history can and do draw sufficient attention to detailed situations which are not in accordance with Marxist economic and social descriptions and to predictions implied in Marxist theory which have been falsified (i.e., Marxism does not work like a scientific theory). Finally, this point is underlined by the amount of time which 'official' Marxist theoreticians have to spend in 'saving the appearances' and by the appearance, operation and institutionalization of official dogmas and dogmatists whose task is precisely to adjust the evidence to the theories (thereby 'saving the appearance' of the truth of these) rather than adjust or even abandon the theories because of the evidence. In other words, institutionalized Marxism is too much like the church to be able plausibly to claim that its explanation of man's nature and position in the world is solely based on evidence scientifically obtained or to be evaluated in a strictly scientific way.

Thus Marxism is not a theory explaining, but a mythology portraying, man's contradictory situation and doing it in such a fashion as to commend certain ways of responding to that situation.

As such it has immensely powerful and revelatory insights about certain features of it. In particular, it calls attention pointedly to the way in which societies 'get themselves organized' in a fashion which is at once exploitive of certain classes and biasedly protective of the interests of other privileged minorities. It further indicates how there is a common network of interests and therefore of power and therefore of manipulation of the social systems by the privileged minorities in their economic links and activities. In other words, it is Marxism which has particularly opened men's eyes to the sociological and economic forces operative in producing exploitation, conflict and contradiction in human society and has made it clear that if there is, or is to be, such things as justice, equality, liberty among and between men, then they cannot be mere functions of the conditions or attitudes of the individual. Further, Marxism has called attention to the existence and powerful role of 'ideologies'. The views held within a society about the organization, morality and habits of the society and how these are situated in and related to the overall nature and structure of things have been shown to be related to (Marxists would say determined by) the privilege and power structure of that society. In other words, the way we are habitually taught to think about the world and our place and behaviour in it in any given society is not a function of truth as revealed to or discovered by our teachers and their tradition but is a function of the way societal power and privilege is distributed and maintained.

As Freud has made us aware of the problem of individual subjectivity and of the possibility that this subjectivity is shaped (?determined) by internal forces and pressures (cf. p. 57 ff.), so Marx has made us aware of what we might call 'social subjectivity' and of how our whole communal way of looking at things is shaped by forces and pressures in and as societies, related to maintaining the status quo for the benefit of those who are chiefly benefited by it. Marx is more hopeful than Freud, because while Freud hopes for nothing more than a therapeutic balancing of tensions within individuals in a perpetually tension-producing society, Marx holds that there is a 'chosen people', the working and exploited classes, who can be empowered by the communist ideology to revolt against the dominant ideologies and exploitations and construct a society which will be open to a classless and non-ideological consummation. It is not to be wondered at, therefore, that Freud is or has been the pre-occupation of the bourgeois and affluent West, while Marx or his offshoots continue to have powerful revolutionary influence in poor countries and among strongly under-privileged classes.

However, while it seems clear enough that Marx has drawn attention to actual features of the shaping of human society and of human beings in a way which is both intellectually and politically stimulating and disturbing, it does not seem that either he or his followers have produced an 'answer' to man's contradictory and exploitive/exploited position. Over-views about the 'real nature' of man's position and therefore of his bondage and of his possibilities of liberation may serve to inspire revolution, but they do not seem to sustain revolution. It is possible to put one's faith in Mao or Castro, not least because accurate information about or experience of what is going on in their spheres of influence is available to very few. However, as there are no sufficient theoretical or scientific reasons for accepting the accuracy or inevitability of the Marxist account of the way things will develop, there seem few solid grounds for supposing that either Mao or Castro have initiated something decisively and definitively better than followed eventually from the efforts of Lenin or than have followed from other leaders, reformers and innovators (however much there is to be learnt from these as from earlier Marxist experiences and others still to come). Thus, while Marx has provided insights into some very powerful and hitherto largely ignored dimensions of human bondage, exploitation and contradiction, it does not seem that he has succeeded in producing or guaranteeing any sure way to human freedom. Marxism can be turned aside into the service of bondage and exploitation at least as well as any other ideology or faith, and we do not need to argue whether this is because of inherent flaws in the nature of Marxism or inherent flaws in the nature of man. At any rate, it is clear that in practice Marxism is at least as ambiguous and contradictory as any other human activity, ideal or institution.

Hence Marx, like Freud, while seeking to explain the human contradiction, only clearly succeeds in adding to the burden of that contradiction. For, on the one hand, he shows by his combination of analysis and insight just how real and ubiquitous that contradiction is and shows, also, some of the sources of this contradiction on the social and economic plane. The contradiction is both individual and social. On the other hand, his very diagnosis, including its presentation in a context of hope, has produced internal contradictions in practice and has become one more instrument of oppression and bondage. It is true that there is still enough heat in the Marxist flame to kindle candles of hope among various oppressed and under-privileged groups. But whether this hope is justified is quite another question. Evidence to date on both the theoretical basis and the actual practice of Marxism can scarcely free us from our reflective pessimism. We may well feel that man as a whole is trapped deeper than ever in an internally and externally conditioned subjectivism (the way he thinks and feels is the product of his psychic growth, upbringing and society) and a network of relationships and inter-actions which either are, or can easily become, dominating and exploitive.

What, then, should be our response to the problem of our subjectivity and to our desire to escape from exploitation and domination into freedom? There is a path of enlightenment offered to enable men to extract themselves from this position by a deeply profound, sophisticated and experienced tradition which does not stem, like everything we have so far discussed, from the West. This is the teaching and tradition of the Buddha. It is clear that in this long established tradition which is so alive and active at the present time, there is an immense reservoir of human experience and reflection. Any attempt to explore the question 'What is man?' would surely wish to take into account the approach and findings of such a tradition. On the other hand, anyone who lives outside, and out of direct touch with, the tradition cannot hope to do any real justice to it without, at least, a great deal of sympathetic study. This I have not so far had the opportunity to pursue. But I feel that some reference must be made to the tradition both because of its intrinsic importance as a sustained and sustaining exploration of the human condition of great age and extent among some sections of the human race and because of the fundamental question which I understand it to pose to all the types of reflection on the human condition which I have been attempting either to appraise or to apply so far.

I am not writing this book from a (supposedly) neutral standpoint, but as a committed Christian who is attempting to explore the challenges posed to our understanding of ourselves and of our race at the present time, and to evaluate the effect of these challenges on my faith and the bearing of my faith on these challenges. As I do write as a convinced adherent of another faith, there is a grave danger that my ludicrously brief discussion of Buddhism on the basis of a very limited acquaintance that is nearly entirely second- or third-hand (i.e., based on discussions and expositions largely by non-Buddhists) will apear to be (and perhaps actually be) super-ficially condescending, and twisted so as to contribute to my already *parti-pris* conclusions. I can only hope that it shows less disrespect to a great tradition to draw attention to it, however inadequately, than to ignore it. Further, I hope also that the effect of the severe limitations of my treatment may be mitigated by the fact that I want to draw attention to one point only, namely the way in which the Buddhist understanding, as I believe, sharply and radically challenges all Christian-type understandings and all Western-type ones. At least to understand something of such a challenge seems to me to throw into clear relief the fact that our ultimate understanding of the bearing of the question 'What is man?' cannot be settled by information, but only by a series of choices or judgments which include judgments about the relative weight and relevance of information to the settling of the question. I shall try to develop this point at a later stage.

Buddhism, then, seems to me to offer us the teaching that there is a way of escape from the problems of subjectivity and the burdens of exploitation and suffering into freedom and peace which it is open to every man to learn and practise. This is the way of enlighten-ment based on the Buddha's discovery (and this is put rather in the terms of my discussion than of the tradition) that the root cause of the human problem is precisely taking the self as subject as decisive for, and definitive of, our approach to ourselves and to the world. We are indeed trapped in subjectivity, with all our burdens of exploitation and suffering, as long as we believe that, and behave as if, the practice of being a subject, being a self, is what is most important to us and essential for us. The desiring self, the judging self, the struggling self, the suffering self, is the very heart and creator of the problem. We can be set free as we learn, by training in various well-tried practices, attitudes and understandings, to cease to act and react as a self, to be concerned with desires or to be attached to the senses and their objects. Thus release can come from the wheel of existence, we can be set free from all the illusions which we normally take as the realities of the world and of ourselves, and there may be the attainment of that liberation and bliss which is referred to as *nirvana*.

If, from a Western point of view, one asks, 'But how does this explain the existence of me and my illusions in the first place?', one misses the point. For the teaching is not concerned to provide a cosmology or give a causal account of the world. The very approach of inquiry, exploration and experiment which is at the heart of the scientific method is held to be near to the centre of the basic human error, which is the source of humanity's conflicts and contradictions. Causal theories are human constructions which carry further the basic human error of treating as ultimately real that which is basically illusory. The teaching is not concerned with the way or the why of *things* and *selves*, but with passing on and making possible that enlightened and enlightening experience which liberates from things and selves.

Now this is clearly a very drastic solution to the problem that man is to himself, but it is also, basically, a very simple one, and the teaching offers a way for one to find out its validity for oneself. Further, it is not an over-view or all-embracing theory in the fashion of Marxism or of any Western metaphysical theory. For it is not based on scientific evidence (at any rate so-called) or on the authority of reason or of revelation (at any rate so-claimed). It is an enlightening discovery which was made by the Buddha (*the* enlightened one) and which can be made by those who follow in the Way. This discovery is made at the very heart of one's being and completely changes the whole understanding of, awareness of, reaction to, being. Hence the teaching is not open to refutation on the grounds that it conflicts with scientific evidence (as it seems that, for example, overall Marxist theory is). Nor can it be dismissed as being 'contrary to reason' or 'contradicted by revelation', because this is to appeal to some externally authoritative criteria of judgment, while the teaching is challenging, from within, the validity of all criteria. Hence the teaching and its evidently powerful livingness seem to me to be particularly pressing and provocative evidence of the capacities of the human spirit and of the way in which it both generates and solves problems. Further, it is to be noted that the solution offered here is not based on information but on experience, experience which denies the ultimate validity of information. No sharper way could, I think, be found of posing the question 'What is man?', for a very decisive line is taken about what is relevant to answering the question. Man is the spinner of illusions whereby he is trapped in the world and in himself (the two fundamental illusions). He can receive enlightenment which dispels the illusions and is, thereby, liberation.

Nothing could bring out more powerfully the experiential reality of man's burden of contradiction and of how he has to choose how to face this burden, choose what he is to make of this burden, choose what this burden is to make of him. The splendour of Buddhism seems to be that it teaches that while this burden does make nonsense of man and his world, there is a way of enlightenment which goes beyond sense and nonsense, beyond meaning and absurdity. (Readers who wish to enter on a serious exploration of the fascinating and important dialogue possible between Western and Buddhist ways of thinking could start out beyond the slight introduction of these few paragraphs by reading Trevor Ling's *Buddha, Marx and God*, Macmillan 1966.)

It does so, of course, by denying the sense of sense or the absurdity of absurdity. Presumably we have to decide whether this is too costly a price to pay. Should the contradictions and conflicts of being human lead us to deny any connection with ultimate values to the various things which are the component parts of the contradictions and conflicts? That is to say, are we to write off the world and ourselves as in any way the sources of our meaning, purpose, values or fulfilment? Does the teaching of the Buddha offer us the only viable way of transcending these contradictions, by withdrawing beyond them?

As I at present understand the matter, there is a fundamental clash between the Buddhist and Christian approaches here. (Let me hasten to add that fundamental clashes in basic approaches do not imply total right or wrong on one side or other of the clash nor deny that necessary and mutually beneficial insights are to be contributed from both sides of the clash. I cannot follow up the matter of dialogue between men of differing living faiths here, although I am sure that it is of the utmost importance. I have attempted a sketch of what seems to me to be involved in such a dialogue in 'The Christian and Other Faiths', published in my *Living with Questions*.) The clash lies in the evaluation of the world and in the evaluation of being a self and in the consequent recommendations about our approach to the contradictions apparently involved in being human. While Buddhism teaches that the liberating enlightenment lies along the way of discovering that the contradictions are all illusions produced by a central illusion, Christianity insists that the component parts of the contradictions are the very stuff of human living and that liberation lies in a redeeming and transforming way of suffering them, living through them, dying from them and rising out of them. While Buddhism seems to cut the knot of our tangled contradictions and conflicts, Christianity claims that the knot is to be accepted and that it can and will be unravelled, provided that the strands are lived with in a certain fashion.

The Christian way of 'placing' the element of conflict and contradiction in being human has traditionally focused round 'the story of the Fall'. I say 'the 'story of the Fall' not 'the Fall' because we must be clear from the beginning of this part of our discussion that we are dealing with mythology (i.e., a story conveying a certain approach, a pictorial and non-literal way of making a point and, possibly, presenting a way of looking at things which claims to illuminate concerning the underlying truth and structure of these things – see further, p. 77 ff.).

We are at present in the process of working our way through four attempts to deal with the question of man's contradictory existence. I think it is sufficiently clear that they are four reactions to recognizably the same situation, however different are the diagnoses and prognoses. (The Marxist and Christian views both conflict and share a good deal in common. The Buddhist view seems, as I have argued, to be fundamentally different to the other three. And so on.) I find this common recognition of a common problem-situation constitutes strong grounds for holding that we do in fact have here a central strand in relation to our question 'What is man?', and I am making my exploration and exposition turn on this point, i.e., I am arguing that an important part of the answer is 'Man is a problem to himself and for himself'. But the ways of understanding and reacting to this problem are very different.

The Freudian and Marxist theories claim to be scientific, i.e., based on evidence scientifically acquired, organized and validated. These claims are spurious but they do not deprive the traditions of thought and action arising from these two men of 'revealing' insights, i.e., of the capacity to direct attention to features of human living which were hitherto not taken seriously and which have to be taken seriously. (On the assumption, that is, that information has to be taken seriously at all.) None the less, the traditions themselves do not provide us with compelling reasons to accept their own over-all interpretations and assessments of what is to be made of these particular insights. To go on from Freudian insights or Marxist illuminations about man's situation to a Freudian or Marxist inter-pretation of man's situation as a whole is a matter of choice, not required by the evidential weight of these insights and illuminations.

When we come to the Buddhist account of the human situation we have a teaching which founds its claim for credibility and truth in a quite different way. We are offered a fundamental intuition which can be shared, a basic enlightenment which can be entered into. This intuition does not marshal evidence and interpretations of evidence to raise questions about the way we choose (through, e.g., drawing attention to the psychological shaping of our motivations) or to throw new light on the way we judge about, and act in, society (through, e.g., drawing attention to our ideological conditioning). Rather it offers and demands a fundamentally new and decisively radical re-evaluation of all choosing and judging as such. The authority of this offer and demand is self-contained. That is to say that its appeal is to interior experience. It in no way depends on exterior evidence because it is precisely exteriority and attachment to exterior things which is challenged. This is a form of 'authority', and a radical questioning of the very status of what it is to exist which is, on the whole, foreign to any form of Western thinking. It is therefore of peculiar importance in making us think and in causing us to think about how we think and who we are that think. It does not seem to me at all sufficient to say that of course such a total denial of the world and self as illusion is nonsense. For even in our brief survey which has led up to this particular discussion we have seen very powerful indications that we either are, or produce, or are on the way to producing, nonsense. Further, Buddhism is clearly produced by and is productive of an apparently very viable way of life. It challenges us to face just how contradictory and un-certain life, as commonly experienced, is and it offers to teach us of a way beyond this nonsense which is based on no external authority and demands no mysterious supernatural grace. I see no decisive way of refuting this teaching. I am fascinated by the simplicity, profundity and radicality of its challenge to 'our' (Western) ways of thinking and, as I get older, I feel that I could easily sympathize more and more with the 'nausea' for existence to which the Buddha was driven. (Sartre and Camus, among others, can tell us about this from a more Western point of view. For a discussion of the bearing of some modern literature on this point see David Anderson, *The Tragic Protest*, SCM Press 1969.) But I cannot believe it.

My profoundest convictions are that it is the stuff of the world which is the stuff of our lives and that our humanity lies in the contradictions – not, as yet, beyond them. I will not treat the world, with its powers, its splendours and its wonderful intricacies as illusion, whatever its complexities or its potential terrors. And I will not surrender the value and the particularity of human selves, with all their intensities of feeling and richness of relationships, whatever their contradictions or their actual sufferings. This is a choice, not an argument; an exclamation, if you will, not a marshalling of information. I shall try in later chapters to draw attention to some information which I feel to be relevant to my choice and the sustaining of it. But I must now make it quite clear that I do not myself find any information which is adequate to dispose of the ambiguities of our human situation. We can only choose how we shall live with this ambiguity, in the light of all the information that can be gained and with whatever help we may decide or discover to be available to us in sustaining the living out of our choice.

This is simply to put in personal but more general terms my own commitment to the Christian side of the clash which I began discussing at p. 66 above and a bringing to bear of those 'Christian and biblical insights' which I was discussing from p. 35 onwards. It is important to notice that while I have been prepared to use scientific-type arguments in putting limits to the validity of the claims of systems based on Freud and Marx, I have not responded to the very differently based and differently aimed 'claims' (not so really claims but teachings) of Buddhism in the same way. This is because, in the very nature of the case, Buddhism is in no way based on what we call science, but raises directly the question of the nature and source of our total understanding of, and reaction to, the world and ourselves. To such a statement, requiring our choice of acceptance or rejection, one can only, if one rejects, reply with a counter-statement and to such a question, one can only put a counter-question. The counter-statement is the affirmation of the value of our world and of ourselves. The counter-question is whether our contradictions are to be understood in the light of our being illusions and the producers of all illusions, or in the light of our being sinful.

5 Not Absurd but Fallen

Many more people will be ready to admit the force of the counter-statement made at the end of the last chapter than that of the counter-question. For what are we talking about when we imply that not illusion, but sin, is to be understood as the key to our contradictions? Here we must finally come back to the 'story of the Fall' which I referred to at p. 38 as the traditional focus of the Christian way of giving an account of, and context for, man's conflicts and contradictions. The source of the story of the Fall is, of course, the third chapter of the biblical book of Genesis, which recounts how the serpent successfully tempted Eve who then persuaded Adam, so that they both ate of the fruit of the tree of the knowledge of good and evil, contrary to God's express command. As a result they were cast out of Paradise, Eve to suffer the pains of childbirth and Adam condemned to wrest a living by the sweat of his brow from the weed-producing ground until he died, 'for dust thou art and unto dust thou shalt return'.

Now, what can possibly be the point or use of introducing something which is so obviously a piece of mythology, probably going back into the fairly primitive mythology of some group of Middle Eastern peoples, as if it could contribute an effective piece of evidence and/or argumentation in a discussion about the nature of man alongside scientific discoveries and theories, reflections on the history of man's treatment of man, reviews of the current problems facing men, considerations of Freudian analysis and Marxist dialectics and a confrontation with the intuitional and experiential teachings of Buddhism? The third chapter of Genesis is, in some ways, a powerful and poignant story, one more symbol of man's awareness of his contradictions and conflicts, but what could it possibly be evidence for?

Here we find ourselves inescapably face to face with the comprehensibility and acceptability or otherwise, of some version of the idea of *revelation*.

We cannot proceed further with our references to 'biblical and Christian insights' as relevant to our problems (as I have already done at some length at pp. 35 ff.) until we have explored and explained this matter a little. For it is central to the question of what weight so-called 'Christian insights' can be claimed to have and the way in which this 'weight' is relevant to points at issue. We come right up against this question at this point because the story of the Fall is so obviously mythological and so unlike the data of science, the information surveyed and marshalled by a Freud or a Marx, or the far more generalized teaching offered by Buddhism. What does it mean, therefore, to place the story of the Fall in the context of revelation? In its biblical and Christian form (or better, forms), the idea of revelation implies that men (some particular men, that is) have been enabled to form ideas, impressions and insights about the nature and possibilities of themselves and of the world under the particular guidance or influence of God. Or, to put it another way round and to avoid an over-intellectual formulation of the idea (which developed more from practice and experience than from theory and reflection), it is held that the pattern of life developed within 'the people of God' with its imperatives, its expectations, its reactions, its corrections and its consequent partially and pictorially expressed world-view, is a response to, and therefore a reflection of, the approach, activity and involvement of God. Hence we have, in and through the life of this people, a revelatory process, a becoming available of insights about the way in which the world is to be received, life is to be lived, hopes are to be directed, and help is to be expected, which would not be available unless there were this God in action and he were concerned to provoke and evolve this knowledge and this response. Revelation, as traditionally understood (and it seems to me that the idea has no useful content and should be dropped if it can in no way be understood in this fashion), implies the activity of God and not just the discovery of men. Thus, what is learned, or pointed to, through revelation is not necessarily what one might expect or deduce. In the biblical tradition there is a very strong element of unexpectedness, of judgment, of transforming newness (I have already made some brief reference to this at pp. 17f). Revelation, then, is understood and received as a source of insights that would not otherwise be available. It is part of, and proceeds from, a positive activity of a God positively conceived of.

Because of this understanding and faith, the people of God (i.e., those who receive and respond to this process of revelation) are bound to conclude that what is given to them in and through revelation will in the end have the last word. That is to say that the 'evidence' of revelation counts for more than all other evidence because revelation, properly received, puts one on to an understanding of, and a relationship with, the ultimate context of everything and the underlying power at work in everything. This revelation is, as I have said, understood as a process, and the process is centred on and experienced through a people. Historically this people is the people who emerge as the Jews, and the tradition, which reflects this process of revelation and which becomes the normative and provocative account of the people's self-understanding of this revelation, is that recorded in those Scriptures which are the Jewish Bible and the Christian Old Testament.

Christians are people who have a fundamental *historical* disagreement (based, none the less, on faith) with the Jews about how this revelatory activity and process of God has come to a decisive focus. Christians hold that Jesus of Nazareth was this focus, that this is sufficiently demonstrated by the shape and impact of his life, of his death and his overcoming death (his 'Resurrection') and that it will continue to be sufficiently demonstrated by the fact that the living Spirit of the crucified and risen Jesus will continue to make an effective faith in him an effective possibility. (I shall try and unpack this somewhat more in relation to our understanding of and hopes for man in the last two chapters.) Thus for Christians the normative record of, and evidence for, reaction to God and his activity becomes what they call the Old *and* New Testaments and the people of God who are directly responsive to and responsible for the tradition of revelation becomes the people who profess and call themselves Christians, i.e., who acknowledge (although they do not live up to) Jesus as this decisive focus of God.

Now all this takes a lot of believing. It is clearly rejected by the Jews for a start, is incredible to all Western atheists, is set aside by Islam as a mistaken and unreasonable form of monotheism, and is foreign to the great religious traditions of the East, among which I have been directing attention to Buddhism. For many (perhaps a greater number than ever before) there just seems no way of going beyond an agnosticism of varying degrees from indifference to interest. Further, there is the clear fact that, in very many ways, Christians are and have been just as ambiguous and contradictory evidence for the truth of their Christian claims as men as a whole are evidence for either pessimistic or optimistic answers to the question 'What is man?'. It is very evident, therefore, that in seeking to bring to bear biblical and Christian insights on the evidence about man and as part of the evidence about man, I am exercising a choice and a faith of a very particular kind. It is particular (i.e., distinct and different) not least in its concern for the particular (i.e., for particular events enabling particular persons to have or to contribute to revealed insights) and for taking this to the logical conclusion (?the absurdity) of holding that the particular man, Jesus of Nazareth, is the decisive focus in history for the understanding of God and his activity. This fundamental intuition of the Christian faith about the possibilities of particularity would seem to be precisely the opposite of the fundamental intuition of Buddhism.

How are we to face and deal with so fundamental a clash and so fundamental an issue? Possibly by concluding that 'fundamental intuitions' of this nature, whatever their content, are nonsense. Man is simply an information-collecting and reflecting animal thrown up by the processes of the universe. In fact these processes neither 'add up' to anything (they do not provide the particularities which are the stuff of human life whereby man has the opportunity of learning of and responding to God), nor do they 'boil down' to anything (they are not rightly understood as illusions from which as from himself, man can escape to enlightenment and peace). They just are and man just happens. The appearance of 'fundamental intuition' is further evidence for the type of answer to the question 'What is man?' which I suggested as a possibility at p. 60, viz., that man is a 'reflective animal who is not sufficiently adjusted to his own reflective capacities, so that he has to hide from the fragmentary and absurd nature of the universe behind unifying fantasies he has contructed for himself'.

Once again (cf. re Buddhism at pp. 68 f. above) I see no decisive way of refuting this conclusion, especially if one decides that absolutely everything is to be settled by information, where the model of information is a scientific one. The evidence is so confusing and contradictory as to suggest a negative conclusion about an overall 'sense'. But, once again, I just do not believe it. It is to be noted that it *is* a decision to settle absolutely everything by information, and a highly selective one at that, as a very limited range of information is available to each one of us. Further, the reflective animal with his maladjustments and his fantasies I am tentatively describing is somewhat more remarkable than a rhinoceros; and even a rhinoceros, as I have suggested, when looked at in a certain way takes rather more 'explaining' than information will permit of. It may well be that it is more reasonably and perceptively responsive to what is offered through being human and what is offered in being human to choose to experiment with the intuition and the teachings of the Buddha or with the discipleship of Jesus, believed to be the Christ.

The fact that one encounters contradictory 'fundamental intuitions' is certainly further evidence of the conflicts and contradictions involved in being a man. But it does not necessarily (I would personally say that it does not at all) diminish the remarkableness of this fundamental intuition-forming animal. What is the world 'doing' throwing up such a 'standing-out' species? Clearly men have felt themselves compelled to ask this question and men do still feel this compulsion. That, at any rate, is an observable and steady characteristic of the human race. No one has, I think, established a *right* to demonstrate that the question is dissolved away, although many have displayed the grounds on which they *choose* to do away with the question. There is no compulsory way out of the question 'What is man?'; we are not *bound* to conclude 'man is nothing but . . .' by inescapable logic or overwhelming information. *Life* may overwhelm us and force this conclusion, but then we are confronted once more with the conflict of light and darkness, the whole agonizing practical question of what help we can get in facing and living with the contradictions, both sides of which can seem so real. Nothing outside us can be held to administer the decisive *coup de grâce* to our human anxieties and human hopes. It is we who succumb or who survive. Men who seek to settle our nature for us by some alleged *force majeure* are, however unwittingly, sharers in the human conspiracy to deprive human beings of their humanity. Why do they do it?

The story of the Fall as understood in the Christian tradition suggests some answer like 'Because men find dependence and responsibility a burden and want to be their own masters on their own terms'. As a way towards explicating this, it is necessary first to notice that although my formulation of question and answer makes it look as if I am claiming the Fall as giving a *causal* answer to man's contradictions and contradictoriness, in fact this is not my intention at all, and could not validly be for two reasons. First, my sentence beginning 'Because . . .' is simply a descriptive comment on the situation the recognition of which led to the posing of the question to which it is an answer. Thus it does not give the *cause* of the situation, it simply offers a suggestion about the *nature* of the situation. Thus it is not a causal answer, but a suggestion about the way in which the situation is to be looked at and reacted to (for what 'caused' men to be like this?). Secondly, if I am to draw my answer from the story of the Fall as reflected on in the Christian tradition, then I am not starting from anything which could possibly be evidence for either scientific or (if there are such things) historical causes. (Whatever may have once been the firm understanding within the Christian tradition of this story.) For, as I have already said, (p. 71; cf. p. 67), it is so obviously a piece of mythology and does not belong to either history or science.

What I am doing is trying to bring to bear a biblical and Christian insight on the contradictions of the human situation. In making *this* attempt I am working from the assumption (explained at pp. 72 to 74 above) that the biblical and Christian tradition reflects the revelatory process (on the initiative of God) by which particular men were and are enabled to learn about and become consciously related to the power and purpose which is at work in the world and about how, consequently, man and his world are to be 'looked at'. Revealed insights are therefore (in the understanding and expectation of faith) about the truth of things, what it is all about and what it can or will all come to, because they are given by God who is understood to be the sense which things will make and the power at work to enable them to make that sense (Creator and Redeemer – see below pp. 81ff.). But revealed insights do not provide either scientific accounts or historical descriptions. They are about ways of looking at the world related to ways of responding to and living in the world, understood as the place where men enter into this relationship with and response to God. The possibilities of looking and responding are realistic (for they are offered by God), but the particular realities which are the stuff of that which has to be looked at and dealt with are the happenings of history and the materials of science. Here there is no substitute for the observation and analysis appropriate to history and science. Revelation provides no substitute for participating in history and science.

One of the chief ways in which Christians have exemplified and embodied the practical truth of the insight proffered them into man's tendency to refuse dependent responsibility and to try to dictate his own terms to the universe lies in their repeated abuse of revelation. The various traditions of Christianity have tended to turn revealed insights into the basis for all-embracing over-views of man and the universe for which revealed and divine authority is claimed. Either science or history, or both, then refute these over-views, discrediting both Christianity and revelation in the process. In terms of their own tradition, however, Christians have the opportunity to see in this the judgment of God, who always overthrows idolatry and who always retains his own initiative and unexpectedness. No human fantasies claiming to explain the world or define its possibilities will therefore be allowed to stand, least of all religious ones which attempt to trap God and his world and his potential collaborator, man, in human systematizations. The biblical tradition does not suggest that revelation or the whole activity of God sets men free from the need and opportunity responsibly to face real uncertainty and unpredictability with the real but limited information which is available to them. I myself am convinced that over-views explaining everything and 'fitting everything in', whether their source is claimed to be scientific, philosophical or religious, are all examples of man's inveterate tendency to play God, even when he expresses it in the form of denying that he is even man.

Thus, any revealed insight has to be related in an open and realistic way to realities as properly rigorous observation is establishing them to be. Unless we have some clarity about this, we, as Christians, cannot bring these insights to bear in any powerful way at all, for we shall simply be mixing up types of explanation or of human activities (e.g., of collecting information and making judgments and choices about our whole context) which are on very different planes. In this connection we are (or should be) now greatly helped by the recognition that much of the understanding of the bearing and burden of revelation is conveyed in the Bible in a story or mythological form. The myths of the Bible are clearly, in one sense, just like other myths. They are stories of a traditional or folklore-like nature which represent the collective way in which a group, tribe or society of men understand their context in the world, face mysteries of their existence and recollect (and thereby compose) their 'history' in such a way as to express this self-understanding and to illuminate these mysteries. Such myths contain no vestige of what we call science and reflect what we call history, if at all, only in a very oblique and highly coloured way. The advent of the scientific era, it is often taken for granted, reduces all such myths to objects of study for the anthropologist and social psychologist. They may, in some cases, also be of interest for their artistic value and for the literary forms they assume in the course of their development.

I have no space to enter here on a discussion of man as a myth-making animal in general or to make any attempt at considering myths as a rich source for studying man's 'comments on life'. We shall have, in the next chapter, at least to remind ourselves of what we are ignoring by giving no proper attention to the depth and provocativeness of man's imaginative life. This omission is, doubt-less, to be regretted, for it would help me to document a good deal further my contention that being a man and, therefore, considering the question 'What is man?' is to do with more than information. (One line of documentation here, incidentally, would be to consider the difference between insensitive anthropologists who 'record' myths and sensitive ones who enter into the life of the people whose myths they are studying. In all fields there always seem to be the equivalent of people who see nothing else in a rhinoceros than one of the largest of the surviving ungulates. It is one more aspect of the puzzle of man that such people always suppose themselves to be the most sensible, realistic and down to earth. Are they hiding from something? Or are they just blind? Or are they right?) However, no discussion can discuss everything, and I have felt it necessary to con-centrate the one in this book largely on man and science and to work outwards from there. Further, my argument does not, at this point, require any extended consideration of the general subject of myth because I am claiming a privileged position for these myths which play a significant role in the shaping and expressing of the biblical and Christian tradition.

This claim is part of the claim about revelation, and the relation of the revelatory process to a particular people, their experience and history, and their understanding of these. I believe the underlying trends and insights of this understanding to be God-provoked and the continuing development of this understanding to be God-sustained and corrected. The form in which these insights and trends are worked out and conveyed will be as various as the tradition actually displays. That is to say that belief in, or conviction about, revelation conveys no *a priori* information about how this revelation is either received, expressed or conveyed. If we discover that the actual vehicle for recording and passing on revelatory self-understanding and relationships (i.e., the Bible within the life of the people) is an amalgam of, for example, myths, interpretative comment on, or re-writing of, a mixture of history and myth and prophetic interpolations of judgment, interpretation, command and hope, then we are warned to be careful about how we attempt to receive and respond to the same insights. But the insights are not deprived of the power to convey directions about how life is and will be and, therefore, about how it should be lived, because the sense of them is conveyed by the telling of stories.

The vital question is about what shaped the telling of these stories. The Christian belief and answer, as I am suggesting, is that God shaped it, working in and through the experiences and responses of this people. Therefore the sense conveyed by the stories, received in and through their context in the whole tradition of which they are a part, is sense about the fundamental pattern of relationships, reactions and processes between God, men and the world.

Two final points are to be noted about this before we go on to apply this understanding of revelation to the Fall and the condition of man. Firstly, the 'sense of a story' is very flexible and has a wide range of interpretations. Hence this sort of sense provides provocations, insights, broad directions and illuminations about perspectives and possibilities, rather than precise instructions and narrowly definitive answers which put a stop to questions. Secondly, if any claim is to be made about taking history seriously, about either individual or corporate history coming to something and eventually producing some sort of satisfying and fulfilling sense, then this has to be done by telling a story which suggests the direction and nature of these individual and corporate histories. This is what Marx does, combining Hegelian dialectic and economic and social observations to do it (the myth of the emergence and victory of the proletariat). Evidence suggests that he caught the habit from the Bible. Again, one has to decide whether such a story can be told. I am trying to explain how I believe, and what is involved in believing, in the possibility of telling a version of the Christian story. I am rejecting the Marxist story as a whole while not denying many detailed insights. Both the stories claim to be about reality and both combine in rejecting the Buddhist judgment that no such story can come to anything because it is an illusion about illusions. If we stick to a belief about reality, which can be expressed only in a story form, then we shall know what the story *really* comes to (if the story conveys true and real sense) only as it comes to it, i.e., only as the real sense of the story is embodied in history and experience.

This, about discovering as you go along what the story really comes to, is a combination of both my points. (Firstly, the 'sense' of a story has a wide range. Secondly, any claim that life or history 'make sense' requires to be put in story form.) It ties up with an earlier point (made on p. 77) at which I argued that the Christian understanding of revelation properly leaves us with the need and opportunity to face uncertainty and unpredictability. We have to give up any idea that revelation gives us any privileged option on what information we shall have to deal with, or on what situation we shall have to face. Neither does it provide us with options of prejudging what will be the outcome of combinations of information or situations. We cannot escape the necessity of living with the information and through the situations.

The purpose of this rather lengthy discussion of revelation has been to enable us to answer the question (posed on p. 71) about what the story of the Fall could possibly be evidence for. I must admit that I have sometimes been inclined to think that the myth of the Fall might be best dropped as one of the most mythical trappings of Christianity, which has been put to some pretty murky uses at various stages of theological history. But there seems such overwhelming evidence that the human situation is experienced as mixed, contradictory and poised between exciting possibilities and destructive threats that one just cannot afford to ignore any hints or clues that seem to be addressed directly to this feature of the situation. Has the story of the Fall been taken up from being an early human mythical reflection on our situation to become part of the poetry and experience of revelation?

In his introduction to the pieces he has collected criticizing the Lorenz–Ardrey type of thesis entitled *Man and Aggression*, to which I have already referred (p. 51), Ashley Montagu says that Lorenz and Ardrey are simply reviving in modern guise the old view of the fallen state of man which says that man's evil acts proceed from his very nature and that he therefore cannot be held responsible for them. He even quotes Paul as if to this effect (*Man and Aggression*, p. xiii). But that is precisely what the story of the Fall and the traditional doctrines reflecting on it do not say. They say rather that man's nature is fundamentally good (created as good and created to be good), that the central practical key to the human situation is man's responsibility and man's choice, and that, while abuse of this responsibility is the prevailing feature of the human situation as we observe it and experience it, this 'fallen' situation (of *abuse*) does not define or delimit the possibilities of being human. God has built in other possibilities in creation and is at work to bring about their fulfilment in redemption.

This last sentence is not, of course, derived from the story of the Fall, but takes us on to the wider context in which this story plays a part. For the story of the Fall is that cameo of the human situation which links together the contradictoriness of the human situation as we experience it with the much broader and more decisive Old Testament statement that human existence is part of a creation which is good and which is intended to fulfil good ends. Thus, in Genesis, the story of the Fall is the way of moving from the opening powerful assertions of the splendour and goodness of creation to the actual history and experience of the human race. Via the Patriarchs and Moses, this history is then focused on the people of Israel as the people of revelation who discover in the experiences of their history the continuing presence and work of the God who created and who creates by sustaining, judging, correcting and renewing.

This sustaining and renewing presence and activity of God is discovered by those who become Christians to be focused in Jesus of Nazareth. In the New Testament, therefore, and in subsequent Christian reflection, the Fall is taken up into the context of the understanding which he provides and inspires. Here the point becomes quite explicit that man is not defined by himself but by the activity of God. For man is not defined nor delimited by his contradictory state but by the activity of God focused and expressed in Christ to take him beyond it. There is no evidence that man on his own can do this. Rather, he is understood as trapped in the abuse of his possibilities and responsibilities. Hence the cameo of the Fall becomes the way of characterizing man's present state with all its contradictions and limitations in such a way that man's existence and possibility is none the less affirmed to be unambiguously good (part of God's creation) and the destiny offered him is declared to be the unambiguous fulfilment of this unambiguous gift of creation (he is the subject of God's redemption). Thus a realistic view of man's state and behaviour which takes a full account of pessimistic possibilities is combined with a clear affirmation of initial goodness and a clear hope of final fulfilment.

But can this optimistic view of man's pessimistic looking situation be sustained? It can, if we can hold that the myth of the Fall has become a valid part of what I have called (p. 81) 'the poetry and experience of revelation'. I have tried to describe how the Fall does fit into the biblical and Christian story which reflects this process of revelation by my use of the notion of 'linking cameo' immediately above. A mythical reflection has become part of a revealed insight. Our authority for taking it as true that man is to be understood in terms of this whole story and is, indeed, part of a story of this sort, is the authority of a faith which has thrown in its lot with the continuing believing and responding people of God and which therefore holds that revelation will continue to give us realistic guidance for receiving and dealing with the realities of human life. This authority is a different one from that to which science appeals or to which Marxism attempts to appeal or to the approach which is implied by Buddhism. This authority is specifically Christian and finds its specific focus and final provocation in Jesus Christ. Nothing but confusion can arise from attempts to hide from this fact. Just as there should be no hiding from the fact that there is no unchosen authority for settling the question 'What is man?'. The information is insufficient. We have to choose what we make of the information and what we take as our decisive aids in this making.

Here we have one more striking fact of the way man 'stands out' of the process of which he is a part. He becomes increasingly aware of what makes him (or how he is made up); he therefore has exciting possibilities of contributing to making himself, but in the midst of all this he finds himself a threat and a contradiction to himself and, yet further, he finds himself faced with the choice of how he is to respond to *all this*. Does he respond in terms of its all being illusion? Does he respond in terms of its all being matter? Or does he respond in terms of its all being material for emergence into co-operation with God? The biblical and Christian story, brought fully down to earth in the life of Jesus, claims to convey the revelation that the proper and truthful response is the last one.

The story of the Fall (in its context of the whole story of creation and redemption) indicates that man has 'from the beginning' been faced with choices of this sort, with a 'serpent-like' ambiguity about his context and his attitude to it. What is typical of him is that he chooses to make himself by himself, to interpret, and therefore in a measure to construct, his environment and himself on his own terms. But this is to deny himself 'Paradise', i.e., to put himself out on his own, to deprive himself of those opportunities of co-operation and response within a far greater context than himself which would provide fully creative work and steadily increasing fulfilment. It is this which is the root of his trouble. Man steadily displays a narrow self-contentedness and a determination to be dominant for his own ends and purposes. In this he supposes that he is developing himself because he is asserting himself, but he has got the context of his development and fulfilment wrong. He has chosen the wrong centre, himself rather than God. Thus the positive point of being a self, the created drives for the development of the self, and the human vocation to have dominion on behalf of God and all men (cf. p. 36 above), all have a tendency to be misplaced and misdirected. Therefore his good potentialities and gifts repeatedly produce bad effects and situations which tend to reproduce their own distortedness. Man's contradictions, therefore, are to be understood and evaluated in the light not of his illusoriness but of his sinfulness (cf. p. 70 above), his self-centred self-assertion.

Now it must be remembered that this is a story giving the 'sense' in which man's situation is to be understood and responded to, not a description conveying precisely accurate and directly applicable information. So 'sinful' characterizes the human situation; it does not provide a label which can automatically be applied to every actual human action or, even, to particular groups or types of action which are singled out, say by ecclesiastical authority or tradition, as 'sins'. This is a difficult point to grasp, not least because it is contrary to the plain sense and practice of a great deal of Christian tradition hitherto, but I think it is essential to a valid bringing to bear of revealed insights on our knowledge of and handling of the human situation today.

On the subject of 'man as a sinner' we have to set ourselves free from the pernicious effects of that abuse of revelation which I referred to above (p. 77). The insight into man's situation as sinful has been persistently expanded (and therefore distorted) in Christian theology and practice into a descriptive over-view which located and accounted for all the actual activities of every actual man. Thus, as it were, an ecclesiastical grid could be imposed on the map of men's behaviour from which competent authorities could read off which men were committing which sins when. Further, the church supposed that it could issue precise instructions to medicine, morals, education and many other human activities. This situation is now exploded, although its effects and vestiges are still very much with us. The human situation has all the biochemical, psychological, social and ideological complications which we have touched upon at earlier stages of the discussion. This particular man doing this particular act may be an example of anything from an over-stimulated thyroid to sheer wickedness and is almost certainly a complex mixture of a variety of conditions. On the other hand, revealed insights are not God-given equivalents on the 'religious' and 'spiritual' side to information and data obtained on the 'scientific' and 'material' side. So religious 'authorities' are in no position to produce precise and independent judgments on human actions. It turns out that the world is a much more unified and homogeneous sphere of action, and responding to God is a much more corporate and experimental activity than the church, at any rate in the West, has for a long time supposed. We are concerned with discerning, learning, and making the sense of a story, not with applying a divine recipe or taking a divine medicine. Revealed insights are indicating to us the shape and direction of the story, our possible place in it and what we may hope for in it and through it.

Thus, to say that man is sinful is to locate his contradictions in behaviour and experience in a particular way. It is to say that they are contradictions and are to be taken seriously as such. They are not to be reduced to some function of man's animal nature. Nor are they to be transcended as illusions. It is to say, further, that they are contradictions for which and in which man must discover responsibility. Further, it is to say that they are contradictions which can be worked through, emerged from, and used as the stuff of creative living by responding to the redeeming activity of God. That is to say that the 'doctrine' of the Fall and of man as sinful deduced, in a variety of forms, from the story is essentially an optimistic doctrine about the positive possibilities of man's life in the world, but the optimism is based on God. The fact that Christians have used it in a highly pessimistic (and at times sadistic) way is evidence that Christians are no more guaranteed exemption than other men from the desire to do better than God and exalt themselves as a standard of judgment while reducing their fellows, all on their own terms.

Thus the sense of the story of the Fall is that, as men and to be men, we must face our contradictions seriously, look for responsibility in them, and respond to the re-creative and redemptive activity of God through them. The actual bearing of this sense has to be discovered in a continuous experiment of living carried on in, and in contact with, the people of God. There will be a whole range of possible interpretations and embodiments because of the flexibility of sense indicated by a story. And also because we are participants in composing the story in co-operation with God. Hence we cannot know in advance just where we shall discover our 'sins', be forced to accept a responsibility which leads us to desire freedom from our guilt and to search for a changing and renewing activity beyond ourselves. In learning how to practise that reassessment of ourselves and our situations which demands repentance (a thinking again which involves a change in ourselves, our aims, motives and relationships) and a creative renewal and readjustment with regard to response and contribution to life, we have to make use of all the information we can get from all appropriate sources. Thus, for example, psychology will alter our view of the sins both of ourselves and of others, for we shall see that responsibility does not in fact 'work' as in a pre-Freudian age it was assumed that it did. But the reassessment we have to work out about 'sins' and 'sinning' does not alter the sense and bearing of the story about man's sinfulness. The working reassessment has to take into account the seriousness of the contradictions as real indications of opposing elements that must *both* be taken into account: the vital issue of the discovery of responsibility and the perspective of response to the activity of God.

A whole book is really required on this one theme, and much work must be done in the Christian reassessment of the sin and the responsibility of men. (For more extended contributions of my own see my 'The Christian Idea of a Free Person' and other relevant essays in *Living with Questions* and 'Responsibility, Freedom and the Fall' in *Man, Fallen and Free,* edited by E. W. Kemp, Hodder and Stoughton 1969.) I am concerned now only to outline a version of the Christian account of man's contradictions, to make clear that it is based on a belief in revelation, to show that it is essentially an optimistic view of man's possibilities related to a full evaluation of the pessimistic features in man's living, to assert that this optimism depends on a view of the activity of God, and to indicate that the bringing to bear of this faith on actual situations and actual developments requires rigorous attention to what actually happens and what information is actually available. The Christian account of man and his contradictions is not an over-view which permits of *a priori* applications or deductions. It is an insight into the way things are moving and therefore into appropriate ways of responding and receiving. But there is no way of avoiding experiment and involvement to find out what it actually comes to.

Thus it may sometimes appear that faith for the Christian offers access to a tradition and life of revelation which is about everything, but tells you nothing about anything in particular. But this impression arises only if you expect to be told the wrong things. The particularities of the Christian faith are to be found in the experiences and relationships of those whose reflections on their experiences produced the revelatory stories, commands and commentaries which compose the Bible. They are secondly, and most decisively, to be found in Jesus of Nazareth. And they are, thirdly, to be found in facing up to the particularities of present questions, decisions and reflections. All this reflects a particular understanding of man which is implied in, but is much wider than, the understanding of man as sinful.

Man is seen as having the opportunity to respond to, search for, and work with God. This is an opportunity and a destiny which, as we have seen, he fights against and again and again rejects, supposedly 'in his own interests'. His destiny and his opportunity, however, are not passive possibilities to be initiated by him alone or a remote goal to which he must strive alone. His destiny and his opportunity is an active God who is present from beginning to end, to evolve from the beginning and the continuing the end which will be the fulfilment. So whether man responds to God or ignores him, searches for him or sticks firmly to what he regards as his *own* affairs, works with God or against him, all is material for God's approach to, search for and working with man.

But this work of God, which continues steadily whether man goes with or against the grain of it, at no point deprives man of his opportunities and responsibilities for searching, responding and collaborating. Hence man's situation is never closed, his searching is never completed, his responses are never finally sufficient, the work which may be creative or destructive is never done. That is why nothing in particular is known in advance. Man has the responsibility and opportunity of living into, and taking a share in, his future.

This is why I see no difficulty in principle in bringing together the revealed insight about the *fall* of man and the biological evidence about the *rise* of man. As I have tried to indicate, the story both of creation and the Fall become part of the poetry of revelation by virtue of the experiences of the people of God in their history and of their reflections on their history. The story form in which these revealed insights were embodied expresses certain general convictions and intuitions by placing them 'in the beginning' of the story, but they are not in fact 'building-blocks' which constitute the beginning of a causal chain. They are insights which refer to the way in which the whole process is to be lived in. I have argued that they are true and vital insights (based, of course, not on argument, but on revelation) about what must and can be taken into account in living in the process. They are applicable at any time and do not, in themselves, refer to happenings at a particular time. They are recommendations to live as if the story were true. Indeed, the sense of the story *is* true, although the story itself is not literally (i.e., historically and scientifically) true. They are available, therefore, to be brought to bear on whatever turns out to be the biological and other evidence about the rise of man. The very doctrine of creation obliges us to take this information with full seriousness. Hence revealed insights and biological and other relevant evidence have to be brought together in order that we may properly consider, face up to and take part in the *emergence* of man. I have drawn attention at various points throughout all the chapters of this book so far to features of this emergence of man which do not reduce but rather emphasize his uniqueness. The question is, what are we to make of this uniqueness, especially as it is so troubled and ambiguous? The answer I would now give is that we are to see in it the emergence of a potential collaborator with God who distorts his possibilities and his responsibilities by choosing himself as the centre of his universe. But even in this he is not defining or delimiting himself, but simply misusing his very positive gifts of self, of choice and of dominion. He can be saved from himself for the fulfilment of himself beyond himself because of the persistent activity of God who creates and saves as the basis of his collaboration.

We must go on, therefore, to see what expansion and concreteness we can give to this answer in relation to the other answers we have seen some reason for giving, and we must take into account the difficulties we have encountered in previous chapters.

But there is one difficulty we have not so far directly mentioned but which ought to be considered at once. If it is a biological fact that man has emerged from the processes of the universe, it is also a biological fact that we all die. Does not death show decisively that man is completely and utterly homogeneous with the universe in every way, and that the overall entropy of the system absorbs him, as everything else, completely without trace? Surely the universe just happens, man just is and in the end there is nothing but inertness. Let us bear in mind this fact of death while we explore a little further some qualities of human life. As we pass to this exploration we may perhaps usefully (?wistfully) note that one of man's unique features from a really primitive stage was that he cared for his dead. Animal animals have no concern for cadavers. Very early human animals buried or burnt theirs with considerable signs of care and concern. Has there emerged here something for which, in some odd way, death is not natural? Is there any possibility of 'standing out' even here?

6 Man on his Way

Despite the great question-mark of death, let us proceed on the assumption, which is my belief, that the sense and direction of the Christian story are basically true, that we may trust, and put to the tests of life and action, the insights about the world, man and God which are thereby conveyed. In this light and on this basis we have the conviction that man and the world are fundamentally to be received and affirmed as good. I propose to discuss in the next and final chapter what content we can begin to give to the notion of 'goodness' here. My meaning at this point is that our Christian convictions and understandings encourage us to be positive, expectant, hopeful, inquiring, energetic and responsive in our approach to the world and ourselves in it. In this spirit, then, let us quickly look again at some of the features of man's life in the world. Anything that we can find to say about or in the face of death will, in any case, have to be picked up 'en route'. For we can address death only with the exclamations to which life encourages us. Beyond death we have no information. The vague whisperings of ghosts and spirits may give some indications of some sorts of occasional survival, but such para-normal phenomena, if they stand up to investigation, can give us evidence only of the prolongation in an attenuated fashion of modes or effects of existence with which we are already familiar. Survival is one thing. A life which had transcended death would be quite another. On this the Resurrection of Jesus Christ is an indication to faith, and an indication of faith to which we shall return. But it remains true that it is in and through life that we learn or lose our faith.

What, then, of the life of man? Consider further the matter and manner of his 'standing-out', to which reference has already been made. Man may be absurd, but it is he who diagnoses this absurdity. Man may be an illusion, but he is an illusion who can perceive the illusion. Man may be biochemically determined, but he is well on the way to understanding and therefore to being able to manipulate the building-blocks of his determined state. Man may be determined by psychopathology, but this he can analyse and realign. Man may be the product of social pressures and states, but the dialectic of these pressures can be understood and co-operated with. The very processes by which men discover their absurdity, illusoriness or determinedness suggest that this is what they, variously, choose to consider themselves to be and not what they are bound to be. They might have been bound to it if they had not discovered it. But if I have the capacity to discover what makes me 'me', I have also the chance of deciding, at least to some extent, what I shall make of what is making me and, therefore, what I shall make of 'me'. Freedom, as an emergent possibility, seems to be thrust upon men, and along with freedom, responsibility. Men are made to stand out at least in the sense that their evolved construction is such that they have evolved to the point where they consciously affect evolution. According to the Christian story they are 'made to stand out' in the broader sense that they are created to be men who shall respond to and work with God. Therefore they are confronted with an obligation to freedom and responsibility which is at the same time their supreme opportunity.

But there is a sense in which it always seems to me that these perennial debates about freedom and determinism, man's reduction to a function of the chemical assemblage of molecules or man's elevation to a 'free spirit', conducted in terms of philosophy and of science, are the least important area for perceiving how man stands out, how he is unique. And this is so, despite all the energy that is put in, and attention that is focused on, them. I am inclined to think that they should be understood and received as *secondary* debates of the utmost practical importance about the emergence of man's uniqueness and the development of his freedom but as quite incapable, in the very nature of the case, of producing any definitive pronouncements about the existence of that uniqueness and the possibility of that freedom. I return to this briefly in the last chapter. Meanwhile, consider some of the many areas which, surely, speak unambiguously of the uniqueness of man, even if that uniqueness is experienced and exercised in ways that are full of ambiguity. (In terms of the Christian story, with the terms adjusted to take account of the biological story about evolution, man may be 'fallen' and the perpetrator of hellish things. None the less, the heavenly image of the divine is sufficiently clearly programmed into his very development to be perceived struggling, often successfully, for emergence and embodiment.)

There is the vast range of human life, styles and achievements, all the richness and complexity of cultures and their varieties. True, there is the dark side to cultures and the historical atrocities in which men of one culture have invaded and destroyed another. But, for the moment, our confidence in the validity of the Christian story's affirmation of the basic goodness of things sets us free to gaze at the good. We shall return to the cost of this later. Review, therefore, in your mind's eye anything that has particularly struck you of the manifold variety and fascination of the products of men from the threshold of their history onwards, whether by way of artefacts or of fashions of communal living or of developments for adjusting to and dealing with their environment. If there is such evocative richness in the material assembled in any good museum or gallery of archaeology or anthropology, what must there have been in practice? And what must there be now to perceive in this or that part of the world? Consider particularly the evidence of inventiveness and of sheer delight in creativity and decoration. Why incise zig-zags on newly invented pottery beakers? Why forge gold into tiny droplets of intricate patterns? Why spend infinite pains in fashioning wood into shapes, representative, suggestive and beautiful? In this, I suspect, men were and are bringing into consciousness the potential vitality and exuberance of the universe manifested elsewhere in our world. As examples of this I have in the mind what seems the over-developed elaboration of plumage in certain birds or colours and shapes in certain fishes. All 'merely produced by evolution', of course. But how splendid for us who can appreciate them! And we men do this sort of thing of our own accord.

Clearly, one of the really dreadful things that threaten us at the moment is the obliteration of so much of this variety and the possibility of some all-embracing grey urbanized technological pattern of living. But before we turn to a final attempt to relate together the real threats and the vivid possibilities and actualities, let us pursue our gazing at the goodness a little further. To cultural richness we must add racial richness. Certainly this takes an act of faith at a time when racial conflict and suspicion is a so prominent and, apparently, growing feature of our world. But it is, surely, an act of faith which is offered to us as the basis for our approach to the conflicts and as the hopes which must be pursued through and beyond these conflicts. There are so many ways of being a man and there is *not* a 'type-specimen'. There is so much variety that there can even be arguments about whether all men really do belong to one specific species. This possibility has been used, and even now is still sometimes used to support dividing races up into groups which can then be arranged in hierarchies of domination and subordination. It seems pretty clear that no scientific evidence supports any sort of division and that this is one more example of man's determination to dominate on his own terms, rather than to co-operate with and receive the riches developing so broadly in and through the world, a determination which always divides men, for 'my own terms' are never wide enough nor flexible enough. Further, it is absolutely clear that any Christians who in any way fall for this way of thinking are betraying the clear sense of the Christian story and the impact of Jesus. Men are one and are intended to become one and grow into one. There is no possibility of distinction of value or rank or domination. But there is every possibility of distinctiveness of contribution. Both enforced separation and enforced amalgamation fail to take seriously the opportunities present in the great variety of men's race and culture. We have an immense amount to learn here, and it seems that the learning will be costly; but we can still be clear about the basic richness and goodness of what is offered to us.

The life of man thus stands out in the wide diversity of the forms which it takes on, both cultural and racial. To this we may add the richness and manifoldness of man's religious experimentation, questing and response. Here, again, are all sorts of contradictions and ambiguities – perversities of behaviour in the name of religion and, indeed, perversities of behaviour directly caused by some aspects of some religion. There is, further, the great problem of the relationship between religious claims to absoluteness and truth and the clash between their formulation and bearing in different religious traditions. But I am arguing that the Christian faith and story, at least, sets us free to see these problems and contradictions as secondary and derivative, part of the 'fallen' aspect of that which is basically good. Therefore, we may search to see what are the good discoveries, the good possibilities, the positive responses which are already available in any field, on the basis of which we are to enter hopefully into the struggles and to seek creatively to suffer our way through the contradictions. Certainly, the growth of the world into a 'global village' gives us tremendous new opportunities for contributing to and learning from the dialogue of religions and faiths. This subject could be adequately opened up only in another book. The point of referring to it here is simply to draw attention to the riches of the religious 'standing-out' of man.

I believe that once we are set free to see that distortions, difficulties, contradictions and unsolved problems are secondary and the material of a response and a search which is primarily given as good and to be fulfilled as good, then any inspection of these riches will show that it is a narrow and cowardly failure of human nerve to write off *all* religion and its insights and experiences as superstition, fantasy and escapism. The evidence, sympathetically looked at, cannot possibly be held to require it, and the *choice* to do so is a fundamental choice being made about the possibilities which are involved in being human. When he worships, is man really responding to nothing, feeling after nothing, making an entirely meaningless evaluation of his existence and his possibilities? Here, in his worship and prayer, his mysticism and sacrifice, his awesome sense of obligation and his joyful feeling after obedience and response, man seems to experience and express his 'standing-out' in a particularly intriguing and provocative variety of ways.

As a religious animal, man stands out both from among the other animals and in relation to his own existence and to existence as a whole, for the very activities and experiences of religion are, so to speak, a reflection upon, a commentary upon and a making sense of what is going on and of my relation to it. This relationship, however, seems to be experienced and understood in an interesting variety of ways which seem to combine in various proportions elements of 'fitting in with' and elements of being 'up against' or of being 'confronted with'. In explaining, in the experiences of religion, the reality around him and of which he is or might be part, man thus seems to sense or glimpse a possibility of belonging, a possibility of not belonging, and a possibility that the whole matter of belonging and not belonging goes or might go very much further than the immediate dimensions and contexts of his own life.

Now, this last paragraph of mine might be nonsense – just a spinning of words which convey nothing in reality because they do not specify *what* is being 'fitted in with' or *what* man is said to be 'up against'. The prepositions are left hanging. But that is precisely the point. The language is left incomplete in an attempt to point to and evoke awareness of a field of human experience which raises and explores the possibilities of our completeness and incompleteness, our belonging and not belonging, our making sense and being nonsense. The *possibility* that the language of the previous paragraph does make sense, or begins to make sense and might be more fully understood and developed, is sufficient to establish the great significance and interest of the richness and variety of man's religious quest. For it indicates the possibility that man stands on the verge of making sense of himself in relation to something very great, far-reaching and all-embracing – or alternatively that he has the choice of responding to and receiving that which would make such sense of him. It is, surely, very likely that the poignancy and bitterness with which the cry of 'absurd' is raised in so much literature and drama are themselves evidence of the fact that a possibility of this nature is glimpsed, and that the conclusion is then reached that the possibility is a fantasy and unattainable. There is no tragedy in the absurdity of what is, in any case, only a trivial accident. The difficulties, contradictions and distortions to be perceived in various aspects of man's religious quest and experience are therefore not adequate and certainly not compelling reasons for ignoring the rich possibilities so far glimpsed through it. Certainly, man both stands out and reaches out. One does not really avoid the question of whether these are meaningless gestures or significant responses by systematically undervaluing the evidence.

Moreover, by making a reference to literature and drama we have now linked up with another range of remarkable activities on man's part. These are all the results of his imagination, reflection and creativity in the sphere of the arts. It is, I believe, clear that at its heart and on its frontiers science is an activity of the imagination, reflection and creativity of man and that there is neither any great contrast nor any drastic conflict between the drive and activity of the human spirit which is at the basis of the sciences and that which is at the basis of the arts. But the effects and products of the sciences have very often been understood and applied, and are still understood and applied by many, in a fashion which implies a conflict between 'scientific activity' and 'imaginative activity'. Such an understanding and application is inhuman both in the sense that it does not do justice to the basic nature of these human activities, and in the sense that an acceptance and application of science which both lacks imagination and ignores the imaginative threatens human development. But this is one more topic which cannot be pursued in this book. Any further consideration of the threat has to be subsumed under the understanding of man as living hopefully with possibilities which have real elements of ambiguity and threat about them which I am seeking to develop in my whole argument. As for the imaginative and creative nature of science, I hope I have sufficiently indicated my belief in this in Chapter 2 and that therefore it is sufficiently clear that I am now discussing the arts as further, and not contradictory, evidence to science about the standing-out of man.

None the less, a consideration of the arts is also necessary as a counterbalance to that actual (although not logical or neceessary) effect of science which tends to make a great number of people value information to the exclusion of anything else when facing questions of real importance. This, as I tried to make clear in my first chapter, is a very dangerous and limiting way of looking at a question like 'What is man?'. For while this looks like a scientific question, it is much more like a poetic question or exclamation (cf. especially p. 15). Without imagination and choice we have no chance of effectively linking any information we may obtain to our real concern in asking this question. Even those who hold that information is everything should at least have the prudence, even if they cannot manage the humility, to look more widely than their own field. Thus, in practice, there are conflicts between what is derived from the sciences and that for which the arts stand. These conflicts are once more, I believe, basically to be understood in terms of our apparently inveterate tendency to insist on understanding things on our own terms rather than to receive opportunities to respond more and more widely to what there really is open to us. We turn therefore to the arts as the particular guardians of man's imagination as well as one more example of man's diverse capacities for standing out in the world.

This turning I can only invite the reader to do for him or herself.

Each of us has his own way of appreciation into the vast fields of achievement, performance and enjoyment here. But let us just recall how great the achievements and offerings are both in extent and in depth. Men devise ways of composing and putting together shapes, colours, and musical notes which result in pictures, sculptures or musical compositions which can again and again focus our attention, deepen our awareness and appeal to our sense in manners which diffuse a richness of appreciation and enjoyment through our whole being. In this creative composition of the visual and musical arts there is a particularly fascinating combination of inventiveness within and mastery over technical means, and inspired insight matching directed expression.

I find it difficult both to be clear about, and to convey clearly, what I wish to say here, but it seems to me that any worth-while work of art is doubly worth while. It is worth while because of the achieving that went into, and which was crowned by, its completion. It does not have to be enjoyed by others in order that its existence should be justified. That it should have been brought into being by the artist's attention, wit, skill, pains and inspiration seems to me to be a creative achievement which is worth-while in itself. But there is a second and surplus worth-whileness which hints at, or perhaps is actually part of, the true glory of the living and developing world of which we have the opportunity to be a creative and co-operative part. This creation of art whose coming into being is, in any case, fully worth while, exists also to be enjoyed by others.

Not only is it the result of the creative attending of the artist, it is a result which has the power to demand the wondering and enjoying attention of others and also to enlighten, enrich and direct their own attending. It is good that it is, there is good in its coming into being and its existence provokes, again and again, an enrichment of good. It is in some such sense as this that it seems to me that man's artistic abilities make him stand out as himself an exclamation of the goodness of the universe, a place where the potential goodness comes to positive realization and therefore a realizer of repeated exclamations calling attention to and contributing to this goodness.

It is true that the exclamations can take the shape of question marks, question marks which may be of an agony as great as the uninhibited glory of some of the straight exclamation marks. But this is only one more example of the way in which the goodness is emergent with great costliness in situations of much ambiguity. Of the glory and goodness of the achievements, including many expressions of sorrow, anguish, doubt and even despair, there can surely be no doubt. Man is capable of bringing the being of things to an exquisite richness of expression and reflection which enriches that very being. We have very little reason other than fear of failure of vision for denying his and, therefore, our own uniqueness.

This uniqueness is underlined if we go on to consider those artistic forms which use words – drama, literature, poetry. Here the products and the contributions may be much more articulate and specific precisely because they make use of language which is the unique gift and capacity which man has evolved to enable the articulation of concepts and the conveying of specific communication and information. I might have been well advised, even in so short a book as this, to find room for a separate chapter in which to discuss language, for we so take it for granted that we may easily miss just what a unique, powerful and essential equipment it is of our humanness. Literature, drama and poetry are all extensions of the basic use and importance of language. As our present subject is imagination and the arts, we may consider this extended use before taking our main theme further by considering language as a human activity in itself.

Consider briefly, therefore, the immensely extended range of possibilities which are pointed to and actualized in the poetic, dramatic and literary use of words. There is much reflection on, speculation about, and anxiety over, the human condition and the world which is the theatre within which the condition is played out. Such reflection can be penetrating or divertingly discursive, provocative or evocative, amusing or repelling. We are enabled to see, hear or imagine things of which we should never have dreamed and that which is under our noses or within our very selves can be thrown into startling relief. In addition to expressions of, and occasions for, anxiety and wrestling, we are confronted with opportunities to share in enjoyment, celebration and sheer play. Sometimes we are invited to wonder at the wonder of it all and sometimes enticed into simple and unaffected rejoicing. We must surely never neglect the human capacity for sheer unreflective and 'irrelevant' joy in our weighing up of 'What is man?' and of his uniqueness and his possibilities. The kaleidoscope of achievements, potentialities and creativities here surely encourages us to see man as part of, and as on the edge of, a mystery of exploration and an exploration of mystery which just cannot and will not be reduced to or by the compilation of information, however exhaustively obtained or completely correlated. The information, rather, has to become part of the exploration, of the possibilities and of the response.

Now, it is in and through *language* that all these possibilities converge. I suggested that literature, drama and poetry were all extensions of the basic use of language. Likewise, without language science would not be possible; indeed, many extensions of language's basic use are to be found in the various scientific fields. For it is the development of language which has made possible those depths and complexities of communication, that accumulation, storage and conveyance of information, that inheritance and tradition of experience, which is uniquely human and which causes and enables men to break out of an evolution that is totally physical and instinctually determined. The possibilities of being human are not limited to what is 'bred into' each generation and by such animal learning in each generation as will slowly, through the processes of selection, affect that breeding. Language provides the means of a living, continuing and developing, distinctively 'human' life which becomes increasingly self-regulating under the impetus of its own discoveries and achievements which are culturally and not physically passed on.

This nature and use of language is another vast field of research and understanding which we are obliged to refer to in a paragraph. But the reference is, perhaps, just about sufficient to draw attention to this very important aspect of, and evidence of, man's uniqueness, which lies, of course, not in the *origins* but in the *development* of language. We are dealing, as always, with something which is in process and emergent, not with something which is totally different and distinct in the beginning, whatever may be the possibilities of the end. Language is the essential tool of man's standing-out. Without language he could not have reflective and cumulative knowledge, and without such knowledge he would be unable to be anything other than a determined product of his environment. With this power of speech and of knowledge he is also a producer of and a conscious co-operator with his environment. He can formulate the idea and activity of himself as absurd, of himself as an isolated and temporarily emergent creative phenomenon in an indifferent universe, or of himself as responding to that which is present and at work in, behind, and beyond the universe in which and out of which man himself emerges. He can, in fact, formulate the question 'What is man?' and do something about it, just as he is enabled to act and reflect in a variety of ways which force him to return with a mixture of inquiry, wonder and anxiety to this very question 'What is man?'.

Language, therefore, not only enables us to formulate the question about ourselves, but also has a great deal to do with that whole standing-out of man in the universe, and even over against himself, which forms the substance, the point and the mystery of the question. We may, I think, usefully draw our inadequate but, I hope, suggestive survey of the positive features of man's uniqueness to a conclusion which is a suitable jumping-off point for our final chapter by considering one more feature of his way of living which is closely tied up with language. Language is man's most important tool of communication, and both communication and language involve the existence of community. Language is both produced by and the producer of community. And human culture and living is essentially a matter of society.

Here we may look at the question 'What is man?' from the aspect of the question 'Where is man?'. So much of any discussion of 'What is man?' is liable to be carried on in terms of generalizations. This is inevitable, but men do not exist 'in general' and 'man' is nowhere to be found. What we find and what we are are men, women and children in particular. We exist as members of our own particular communities in our own particular contexts for our own particular limited span of life and time. As such, we share in very varying degrees in the riches of human achievement which I have been pointing to as clear marks of the way man stands out in the world. Likewise, the existing possibilities which science offers to man are very variously 'offered' to 'us' in our various particularities. What is true of 'man' in these vast fields of achievement and possibility – science, arts, technologies, works of imagination, creativity and enjoyment – is not true in anything but a fraction of its entirety of any man in particular, and would seem to be actually false of many particular men, women and children whose lives are grossly under-privileged and deprived.

But, in the spheres of language and community, all men at least begin to share in that which is at the basis of human possibilities and from which the possibilities and the achievements extend. More than that, of course. In their particular communities, all men share in possibilities of suffering and of joy, of living with and speaking with their fellows, and of dying. Thus all men share, in their particular ways, in those relationships of common living which are the very essence of being human. The most 'unsophisticated' villager of the most poverty-stricken Indian village or the most remote jungle hutment, whether in Amazonia or the Congo is, in his or her home and family, quite as human and quite clearly as human as other men, steeped in science, art and culture, are in theirs. Some might want to argue that directness and interdependence of human relationships is more likely to be found among the former cases than the latter. But this we cannot pursue. What we have to dwell on is the essential humanity of human relationships.

The point I am trying to make here requires help rather from art than from science, for in appreciating it neither information, measurement nor analytic description can replace experience and awareness. There is alarmingly little connection between describing 'warm affective relationships within kinship groups' and being loved. Despite my respect and admiration for science and my absolute conviction of not only its essential necessity but also of its great wonder, I am sometimes tempted to judge that, as practised, it is more often an activity designed to escape from reality than to come to grips with it. But here we are back to the apparently inescapable ambiguity of all human activity, an ambiguity which the Christian story and faith, as I am arguing, assures us, does not remove the essentially good basis and ultimate possibility of this activity. None the less, this pervasive ambiguity, not to say perverseness, does seem to make it often easy and even oddly attractive to 'miss the human point'. It is so much easier, apparently, to generalize about human beings than to deal humanly with one's neighbour and oneself. Doubtless this is basically connected with the cost as well as the glory of becoming human which we shall finally have to face before we close our argument and the book.

But what do I mean by 'the essential humanity of human relationships', 'the human point' and 'dealing humanly with one's neighbour and oneself'? I do not think I have to be very specific about this for the purposes of the particular argument, for I am trying to point to a whole dimension of being human of which we all have an awareness even if we do not know always what to make of it or what we may fully hope of it. It is a dimension to which I can point by giving two (necessarily personal) illustrations. The first is the effect of a good collection of photographs of the human face, both of faces on their own and of people looking at one another. What entices, fascinates and provokes is both their infinite variety and their mysterious resemblance. There is something characteristically and poignantly human caught by the photographers in such a variety of guises. It is this quality which invites our recognition, encourages our response and very often provokes our compassion or even our guilt, because we are reminded of 'inhumanities' in which we have some share or which we seem helpless to prevent or assuage. Our guilt, our compassion, our recognition and our enjoyment are all forms of awareness of what it is to be human and to behave humanly. Our great limitation is that in actual practice we live up to this and into this for so little of our time with the fellow humans we actually encounter and for whom we have any direct responsibility. Further, the range of our practical sympathy is so small that we soon and unwittingly cross the threshold beyond which human beings are, for us, 'less than human'.

(It seems to me that the good news conveyed in and through the Christian story and by the actual living, dying and living again of Jesus Christ is precisely that God never ceases the costly work of enabling that 'threshold' to extend outward in the case of every man so that in the end there is the hope of all men being enabled to act fully humanly to all men and thus become fully human together. In other words, that love is at work to make love fully possible and fully enjoyed. I am not sure that I can say much more than this or go much further than offer it as a parenthesis which I believe to be a glimpse into that which ultimately illuminates and enlivens the whole. But I shall have to try to make the last chapter expand this a little.)

My second illustration pointing to 'the essential humanity of human relationships' is drawn not so much from the field of discovering something essentially human in a wider and wider range of human beings but rather from the experience of discovering deeper and deeper possibilities in relation to particular human beings. I have in mind that deepening intimacy of relationship in which two people discover one another and in the discovering actually contribute to that which is to be discovered in one another. He or she becomes known and experienced more and more as himself or herself and thus more and more worthy of his or her own proper and personal name. Indeed, it becomes clearer and clearer that only the distinctive proper name is adequate to refer to the reality and mystery of that person. Nothing purely descriptive will do, because all descriptions partake of generalizations, and although they will be both necessary and possible, it becomes more and more evident that they are not sufficient. What I am seeking to point to here is the discovery and building up of personal identity in a mutual inter-change, inter-action and enjoyment. This is something peculiarly human, and it is neither confined to nor guaranteed by any particular level of either privilege or deprivation. However, the recognition of its existence, or of the possibility of its existence, among all men surely demands a human fight against deprivation and a human struggle to share privilege.

For surely the question of man does come to a focus here. Here are these human possibilities reflected in so many human faces grouped in so many different communities at so many levels of economic existence and under such a variety of cultures. Extending out of this vast complex of living, suffering, enjoying and dying human beings, some human beings have developed and are developing exciting possibilities of science and technology which match up to achievements of amazing brilliance, diversity and depths in the fields of art, music, literature and the general enjoyment, exploration and celebration of life. Many individuals never enjoy these possibilities, many groups are grossly under-privileged in relation to these possibilities and achievements, and many of the possibilities have threatening aspects which could add catastrophically to the contradictions of human living. Moreover, none of us in particular enjoys all the achievements of man in general and, in any case, we all die. What, then, is man?

Mankind is a constellation of the points where the experiment of the universe begins to come to a consciousness of itself and therefore becomes ready to learn that this experiment proceeds from, and is intended to progress towards, the experience and the expression of love. To put it more shortly and in a manner which will probably seem more comprehensible, but will sound more sentimental, *man is the emergent lover who has everything to learn about love*. This, I believe, is a legitimate way of focusing what we can learn from reviewing the possibilities, the achievements, the contradictions and the commonplaces of human living in the light of the understanding offered by faith in Jesus Christ seen as the focusing point of God's revelation and activity. I attempted some explanation of this understanding in the last chapter and I am now returning, in the light of the material reflected on in this chapter, to the notion of the emergence of man in the midst of the world in relation to God which I reached before (cf. p. 88).

The notion that I am now putting forward is that we should understand ourselves as at the centre of the present fragile and ambiguous flowering of the experiment of the universe on earth, an experiment which is in no way completed but must be understood as being very much in process. This is to understand the universe as the creation and the creative activity of the God who is universally at work, but also particularly revealed through the experience of the people of the Bible and particularly focused in Jesus Christ. That is to say this is an understanding of Christian faith and an unambiguous assertion, in the light of that faith of the uniqueness and the potential cosmic significance of man. I have argued that the uniqueness resists all attempts to reduce it based on evidence and information alone. What is really at issue is whether the uniqueness can have any unique significance. The answer to this is a matter of choice and of faith. I make my choice because of my faith in God through Jesus Christ, and I seek to explicate and activate the meaning and bearing of this choice.

In this connection I think it is worth remarking that it is not self-evidently absurd, as is sometimes alleged, to see any cosmic significance in the uniqueness of man because of the vast size of the universe (or universes). Where else has such a flowering yet been found? There is great excitement every time some traces in a meteorite from outer space or some configuration of cosmic dust suggest that elsewhere there might be 'life', i.e., organic matter. But what difference would it make to the significance of our flowering to discern the possibility of it being elsewhere also? Perhaps it might enhance it. I do not see how it could reduce it except in the eyes of those who want to run away from the possibilities and responsibilities of this uniqueness. Further, the traces have not so far suggested, at the most, anything more than the very lowest form of organic life or even its inorganic components, which are about as banal and desolate as the surface of the moon. There is something almost pathologically odd about our desire to reduce ourselves away, but there is so far no real evidence that the universe offers us any corner in which we can escape from our uniqueness. It may well be that our real worry is whether this experiment which has, so far, produced us, can possibly come to anything ultimately. With something where the uniqueness, the glories and the beauties are so poised on a mankind of such fragility, contradictions and incompleteness, can we really dare to believe that man is the emergent lover in the experiment and experience of the universe? Are we, each one of us and all of us together, the experiment of emergent persons in a process which can realistically be received and understood as the experiment of an almighty and invincible love?

Let us see, finally, what we can make of the understanding of man as an emergent migrant who is on his way to building and receiving his identity and his community in response to a God who is love.

7 Fellow Traveller and Destination – God

In facing the question 'What is man?', we have not only come up against the difficulty of deciding what information arising from what areas is relevant to this question. We have also the difficulty of deciding what the bearing of this information would be on the question. But, further than this, we have had to call attention to so many contradictions in the life and behaviour of man and in his assessment of, and reaction to, this life and behaviour. But even these difficulties are not all! There is also the difficulty of relating any understanding we might decide was permissible, possible or powerful about man in general to the living and dying of any man in particular. It may be possible to entertain the notion, vision and hope that man is a creative artist with capacities for love in whom the universe begins to become aware of the sense it might make, the meaning it might develop and the fulfilment to which it might respond. But what is that to me who mourn the death of my starved child, or to me who eke out a depressed existence in the isolation of a bed-sitting-room from which neither my economic capacities nor my psychological make-up will allow me to break out, or to me whose life is dominated by the hours of shift work, the need to meet the hire-purchase commitments and the uncertainties of family accommodation in an area scheduled for re-building? Whatever man may be, I can only live as me.

Now, if living as me is a problem to me and, maybe, to other people, which is sufficiently disturbing, distressing or provoking to keep me asking 'Who am I?', either consciously or implicitly, then three possibilities may confront me (cf. particularly Chapter 4). Perhaps there is no answer in any way commensurate with the question and I can only live with this absurdity until I cease to exist. Perhaps, however, I can destroy the question by learning how to be rid of myself and to cease to experience my existence as *me* (cf. the Buddhist way). Or perhaps the question indicates not my absurdity nor my illusory concern with myself but that as a self I am incomplete, but with hope of completion, meaning, fulfilment. This last is the understanding and hope offered by the Christian faith, an understanding and hope offered very explicitly in the face of a serious and realistic evaluation of the dangers and damage of repeated and misplaced self-assertion (cf. Chapter 5). But how does our Christian faith and understanding enable us to face the interlocking sets of problems involved in confronting the question 'What is man?' which we have just summed up in the first paragraph of this chapter? It seems to me that the way in to a final attempt at summing up the possibilities here lies via considering the last of our difficulties, viz., how can we relate any answers to the question 'What is man?' to the answer we can encourage anyone of us to have to the question 'Who am I?'. That is to say, how are we to understand the particularity of the existence of each one of us in the light of all that is and seems to be involved in the existence of men in general and *vice versa?*

The Christian story as it is sealed, vindicated and directed by Jesus offers the faith, the gospel and the understanding that the clue and the conviction is love. This is so because there is a God and *he* is love. This means that the universe is not a totally self-contained and exclusive system, independent of everything but itself. Rather it (or, if the facts require it, 'they', for the understanding of God is infinite and as capable of embracing any number of universes as of embracing one) is the experiment of a power, presence and purpose who is rightly understood in terms of love. Since the power is infinite and is indeed God, this means also that the experiment is an experiment into the meaning and possibilities of love, so that neither 'God' nor 'love' are closed terms whose meaning we know. Rather, God is an existence, and love is a possibility which it is the whole meaning and purpose of man to enter into. All is an experiment whose meaning is to be discovered in experience. But the Christian understanding is that man is 'the image of God', i.e., that which has evolved within the experiment as the reflection and reflector of God who can respond to and collaborate with the love who is the basic source, sustainer and completer of the experiment. As the emerging responder to and collaborator with love, man is to be understood also as the sharer in the fulfilment of that love. Hence, as the emerging image of God, man can know enough about the meaning of both 'God' and 'love' to take his guidance and his hope from faith in the God who is love. What this *will* mean has, as I have already said, to be discovered in experience as the experiment proceeds. But what it will certainly mean is that the potentialities of 'man', displayed and being discovered in the general and total history of man, are potentialities of the total history of man, are potentialities of the total and universal experiment in which every particular man is ultimately offered a full and personal share. For the experiment is fundamentally the sphere of the activity of the God who is love, and a love which is universal can hold together all that a universal love brings forth and offer it to every particular object and source of love. Only love could fulfil everything in particular and everything in general in a mutual fulfilment.

But as part of our attempt to see a little further into what this might begin to mean, we have to consider how talk of the universe as the experiment of love can be maintained in the face of the actual experience and history of men. I am sure that no faith in, or vision of, the universe as such an experiment could be possibly credible without reason to believe in a crucified God, just as no living as part of such an experiment could be conceivably viable unless there were grounds for believing that we are called to share an experiment with a God who suffers the experiment's cost.

This is where our belief about and faith in Jesus, and therefore in God, is absolutely central to the answering of the question 'What is man?'.

Since one of the pieces of information we now quite clearly and firmly have about man is that he is homogeneous with the universe, it is now also quite clear that the questions which man raises about himself are questions also about the world. The 'building-blocks' (cf. Chapter 2) of man and everything else are precisely the same. Hence the questions 'What is at work in the world?', 'What is man?', 'Who am I?', are all bound together in a chain which is both physical and logical. (The same material is involved and our thinking about them must be connected up.) Therefore, if 'What is man?' is to be a question and exclamation which has an answer and a response which measures up to the heights and the depths of the overtones and undertones which we have detected in it during our survey and discussion, the answer and the response will be concerned not just with man but with everything.

Here we are back to the rhinoceros, or rather to that of which I attempted to make the rhinoceros both an example and a symbol. It is the universe and all things in it, both in their particular existences and in their existence as a whole which is the mystery – or else simply an agglomeration of 'data' ('data', of course, which are not really given but just happen to be there) which can be reduced to information and *nothing more*. Man is not unique either in his 'building-blocks' or in his being mysterious. He stands out, rather, as being the mystery who is capable of appreciating the mystery. There is absolutely no evidence that the rhinoceros is in any way bothered either by the fact that he is, or by the fact that he is a rhinoceros. But we ask 'What is man?' and 'Who am I?'. Thereby we focus our awareness that the whole of existence is a mystery – or a nonsense. This ambiguity has been with us throughout our discussion just as it is with us in our lives. It is reflected in man's attitude to the rhinoceros as to everything else. We can exterminate the rhinoceros and so show ourselves totally indifferent to the mystery; we can treat the rhinoceros as a deity or totem and thereby shut up the mystery in the limitations of idolatry; or we can begin to see the rhinoceros as part of the worshipful possibilities of the whole universe with which we are bound up as in one bundle of life. We can and indeed do treat other men and our own selves in a similarly ambiguous and contradictory variety of ways. Hence the fundamental question as to whether there is a mystery at all and whether there are any real, lasting and humanly satisfying possibilities of response and fulfilment.

It is in this connection that I want to take up my suggestion (p. 22) that as man 'empties the universe of mysteries, so he gets nearer to being able to appreciate, or at least being forced to face, the mystery'. I hope I have sufficiently illustrated this by my further discussion and by the point I have just been making above. We can eliminate all sorts of puzzles by the information we experimentally obtain. Thus 'mysteries' about, e.g. the migration of birds (cf. p. 24) or about why some babies are born deformed and others not are being steadily eliminated. But we are thus given more and more opportunities of 'confronting something of the quality, of the diversity and of the richness of texture of the universe of which we are parts' (cf. pp. 22 ff.), and this in a manner which confronts us with the demand, 'What response shall we make?', 'What responsibility shall we assume?'. For, as I have already argued, to be able to decode the universe is to be faced with the responsibility of encoding and the risk of miscoding.

Thus the steady elimination of mysterious puzzles brings us, more and more, face to face with the human mystery (or nonsense). What is there to respond to, and what is there to be made something of, by man in the universe?

Now the Christian answer is the love of God. And one way of unpacking this answer, which seems to correspond both to the biblical story focused in Jesus and to man's present situation and possibilities in the world, is to describe the universe as the experiment of love within which man emerges as a collaborator and migrant on his way to the fulfilment of identity and community within the development and the consummation of that love who is God. The experiment, however, seems to be threatened with the possibility of total failure (man will blow himself up, starve himself out or pollute himself to death) and to be full of endless particular and partial failures (the miseries of individuals and civilizations, let alone their deaths). How can we believe that the fundamental context of our human living is love at work on a universal scale and with particular concern?

This belief, practice and hope is the offer of God in Jesus Christ. For myself, I can see neither any inescapable external compulsion to accept this offer, nor even any externally compelling evidence that such an offer really exists. None the less I am persuaded that the offer is there to kindle our faith and not to indulge our fantasy. We are offered Jesus to see in him and to receive from him the possibility of the universe. As I have argued throughout, clearly we have to choose what we regard as the most significant and decisive clues in answering the question 'What is man?'. The human situation is such that none of the answers that are given, nor the clues that are offered, compel us to accept them and leave us no option. We have to choose in what direction we will make our response and only experience can show us whether our response is met and reciprocated or not. Herein is peculiarly concentrated the uniqueness and the mystery of man, his glory which can become his shame but may simply be his absurdity. He can discover himself to be free to deny the significance of his existence, to assert its absurdity or to look for the fulfilment of his existence in response to the possibilities of a God who is love. But even the discovery of this freedom is itself an emergent thing. By no means all men are aware of these options, and for many men no such options seem open, for they are conditioned by their society or tradition to take a received view of themselves and the world in which no option of freedom can be consciously conceived of.

So we have to ask once again how what is true of some men is related to what is available to all men in their various particularities. Here the Christian answer would seem to be that the freedom to choose what one shall respond to and look for in the world and in oneself which is so agonizingly or exhilaratingly experienced by some men is a reflection of what is ultimately offered to all men. They are offered, or are to be offered, the freedom to be themselves. That is to say, they are developing into beings who are not compelled by conditioning, nor bound by responses, but who are gradually brought to the position where they make the response of love to the offer of love and thus freely become themselves by the free giving and receiving of themselves.

Now this is a vision of emergent possibilities partly enjoyed, partly misused and partly quite unattainable as yet. The vision comes from the offer of God seen in Jesus, an offer which by its nature could not be compelling, for if it were it would destroy its own nature. For this is the offer of universal love, enticing and encouraging the emergence of particular selves to the point where they can respond with freedom to the freedom of that love. On this understanding, all the ambiguities of man's life and all the contradictions of his living are to be seen within the context of this universal experiment of love concerned with the emergence of persons who can and will love on their own account, which is the only way in which love can love.

The reason that what I have called the 'offer of God seen in Jesus' encourages such an understanding and vision as an act of faith and not as an escape of fantasy is that the consummation of the life of Jesus was his crucifixion, that is to say his suffering and his death. Thus, to see the offer of God in Jesus is to see God offering through and in suffering and in suffering and death. For those of us who share the faith that first produced Christian discipleship, viz., that

110

not death but life had and has the last word on this suffering and death, it thus becomes clear that the way of God in the world is fully identified with suffering and death. Hence we dare to believe that God is neither indifferent to nor detached from the sufferings, ambiguities and contradictions of the world. Rather we see him as involved in and part of these sufferings. Thus we can believe that the crucified Jesus is also the crucified God and that we are part of, and have a share in, a costly experiment with a God who suffers this cost. (I have tried to say something more about this in 'The Suffering of God' in my *Living with Questions*). Hence, to believe that the world can be lived in by man as a fellow partner in an experiment to do with the emergence and fulfilment of love is not to underestimate the cost nor to ignore the contradictions. It is to put together the living and dying of Jesus, via the conviction and experience of his continuing life (his resurrection), with the actual experiences and processes of human living in the world.

From such a faith, understanding and vision it is clear that man has a *future* and that this future is what finally defines, determines and fulfils him. Further, it is in this future that the questions 'What is man?' (in general) and 'Who am I?' (in particular) receive one and the same answer. This is what I believe and this is what I am going to try and explain, or at least point to. But I must confess that when I come to think about it in a reflective and discursive way I find it very hard to believe. What revives, renews and sustains this way of receiving and responding to man's life in the world and my life as a man is a combination of two pressures which are, I believe, from one ultimate source.

The first is the pressure of the multi-faceted splendour and tragedy of human living if it is attended to and entered into, rather than surveyed, catalogued, categorized and commented upon. The information available and the data to be surveyed are essential but are not sufficient. The pressure comes decisively from human living, human faces and human encounters and not from the constituent and supportive facts. I will not readily believe that a child dead of starvation is simply a statistic of famine or war and that the love of the bereaved mother which makes both the death and the mourning so terrible is simply a particular case of the physiology and chemistry of an interrupted maternity cycle. ('Cows when deprived of their calves during the first x days after birth show considerable signs of distress by incessant lowing, etc.') As I have said above (p. 104), the universe does not really offer us a corner into which we can escape from our uniqueness, and it is exceedingly difficult to reduce to statistics or physics the tragedy of death, the joy of birth or the poignancy and power of love. To this pressure, then, I find conjoined the pressure of the impact and story of Jesus as it is presented against the background of the biblical people of God and through the community of continuing believers. These two pressures combine to move me into belief in God which I experience as a way of receiving that human life which I share with all men and a way of living into the realities and the possibilities of that life. The universe as a whole and each particular experience of life within it is to be received, responded to and wrestled with as alive with the possibilities of God's bringing to birth, process and development that which can become a responsive and creative part of his love. Neither the existence of God nor the divine possibilities of human beings are so utterly incredible as we are sometimes led to believe. But if there is a mystery of love in the discovery of which God and man are united, it would seem to be an infinitely costly combination of the fragile and the indestructible.

I do not see that anyone has the right to pronounce on this cost (who can weigh up the meaning and experience of human suffering or the identification of God with this?). It is simply a question of receiving an opportunity to share, however minutely, in the cost which one hopes is also part of the gain. For perhaps it may be said that the cost is a measure of the worth. The bringing to birth and to a perfect development of lovers who can share in an infinite love would clearly be no light matter, whether as to cost or to achievement or to worthwhileness (or should I say 'as to worshipfulness'?). At the very least, to speak of the love of God realistically in relation to such a world as we have and as we produce it is to express one's reverence for man as he is in the light of man as he might be. But in the light of Christian faith it is far more. It is to dare the claim that what man might be already exists. God, into whose image man is emerging, is, and he is love. Man's struggle is therefore a response and man's life is therefore a gift.

Not that it therefore appears what we shall be. Since the future of man is God and God is love, this future is an open future. The possibilities of the experiment therefore have infinite room and have to emerge in the course of the experiment. Man has the responsibility and opportunity of both living into, and taking a share in, the shaping of his future. The risk which God has taken and continues to sustain by the cost which love must pay is the risk of real newness, the risk, that is, of genuine, divine and loving creativity. Of this risk man is the benefactor and in this risk man must share.

Thus, while what man might be already exists in the sense that God, who is the power, purpose and presence of universal love, is the constant factor in the situation, who pre-exists every situation and lies ahead of every situation, none the less the form which the dependent and emergent lovers will take when they all come together in the fulfilment of the enjoyment of this love who is God does not exist. It is being prepared through, and built up out of, the processes of the universe or universes and the achievements, sufferings and experiences of human living within the universe. Because our future is God it can be taken absolutely realistically and seriously, but the God who is revealed to the people of the Bible and who is vindicated in Jesus takes history and therefore creation absolutely seriously. Hence the place where men encounter the possibilities of this future and play their part with regard to it is in the present, in their present particularities. Here we have both the hope of receiving, and the responsibility for shaping, our future which is also God's future.

I said, when raising the question of racial diversity (p. 92) above) that 'there are so many ways of being a man and there is *not* a "type-specimen" '. The immediately foregoing discussion, I believe, reinforces that point. But it may be thought that a Christian should maintain that Jesus is the 'type-specimen' of man. I do not think, however, that the universal significance of Jesus can usefully be put in that way. Rather, he is to be understood as the particular embodiment at a point in human history of that universal form of love which is the reality of God and the reality into which men have to emerge and grow. He certainly embodies the future of man in history, but he cannot express it, for that future has to be built up and entered into by the continual working of love from God and in man. The full expression of this future lies only in God and beyond history, for there is not sufficient room in time and space to fulfil the human possibilities that emerge in time and space. This is, perhaps, the main basic reason why the question 'What is man?'

can have so many answers, so many confusing answers, and so many ultimately unsatisfactory answers.

Theology and faith must not attempt to give a complete answer either. For theology, if its basic faith and insight is true to itself, must understand in the particular terms of faith what all deeply perceptive human beings have again and again understood or at least glimpsed. This is that no solution to our various problems and no answer which can now be given to the question 'What is man?' is or can be human enough. For man is to be defined and fulfilled only in God. Thus the fulfilling future of man lies in the future of God beyond history, time and space. But our contact with this future lies always in our particular 'nows' just as our guarantee (or, perhaps better, evocative promise) of this future lies in the particular historical person of Jesus.

Hence I do not believe that the question 'What is man?' can be adequately faced up to in anything other than a transcendent context of a God and of a universal love which embraces and interpenetrates the particular. Further, I do not see that there can now be any satisfactory answer to the question. Indeed, no attempt must be made to give one or the very point of the question will be destroyed. For man is an open question, directed towards a future of love through present possibilities.

Since, in the Christian understanding, the question has an ultimate answer which has to be received from the infinity of God, although it is contributed to by man himself, it seems to me clearly implied that man is offered the possibility of eternal life. That is to say, that while the work of love is begun in time, its fulfilment lies in the eternity who is God. Of the nature of this fulfilment, of course, we know nothing, although we may guess something through our experiences of the depths of love. Thus we really have nothing to say about that which is symbolized and pointed to by such phrases as 'the resurrection of the body and the life everlasting'. None the less I am sure that against 'the great question-mark of death' to which I referred at the end of Chapter 5 and the beginning of Chapter 6, we have to place the exclamation mark of phrases such as these. If we receive the hope of love, then we receive also the promise of love, and if God is love then those who are learning to love may expect that this promise is not in vain. Again, the impact of Jesus and the conviction among his disciples both then and now of his resurrection combine with the impression of the quality and depth of both life and love to give us this hope of the total and final affirmation of life in which we shall, as ourselves, have a share. In which, indeed, we shall become fully ourselves only when we do so share. What is unfinished now will be finished then; what is now uncompleted promise will be completed then. (I have tried to expand a little more on the meaning of resurrection with regard to our future in 'What is There to Hope For?' in my *Living with Questions*.)

Such talk is clearly unmitigated fantasy if it is uttered in isolation from the whole of life and applied out of a vacuum of experience in the desperate hope of stopping the ugly and bottomless pit of death from swallowing us up. Death cannot be confronted with words isolated from experience. But if we have begun, through life and because of life, to trust that which is at work in the world, in its heavens and its hells, in its crucifixions as well as its resurrections, in its sufferings as well as in its joys then we may perhaps begin to believe that Jesus is more than a symbol of the value of life and that he is rather the sign of a power of life commensurate with that value. Hence we may hope that resurrection is a universal possibility and that man was not made for death but for immortality.

But this is an immortality which has to be received in a future which has to be grown into now, and for which man has now some urgent contributory responsibility. It is here, I believe, that we return to the relevance of the protest, criticism and disillusion of youth in relation to the question 'What is man?'. In a youth which is concerned enough either to sit in or to opt out I believe we have one powerful voice of the conscience of the future complaining bitterly to those of us who have settled for the past or are complacently content with the present. I do not say that the content of the conscience is clear, necessarily helpful or generally right. It is the form and tone of the conscience which is so important (cf. my lengthier discussion in Chapter 1 from p. 14 onwards). It cannot be human to be content with things as they are. It is positively inhuman to ignore and accept the continuance and proliferation of injustices, inequalities and insensitivities produced by structures and trends established over the years. It is monstrously and obscenely inhuman to live not only richly but also with self-righteous satisfaction off these states of affairs. To raise, for instance, the cry of 'Law and

Order' in the name of decency, humanity and democracy when there is no readiness to pour money and effort into helping those who live in the indecency of poverty and oppression to be real participators on equal terms in the running of our society is to act with deep inhumanity. Order we must have if we are to regulate our increasingly complex societies for potentially human living, and some laws we desperately need for our guidance and, up to a point, for our corporate control. But truly human law and an order which permits the emergence of truly human living is defined by the future not distorted by the past, for it is in the future that there lies man's fulfilment. Hence we must heed the voice of youth as the conscience, however inarticulate, of this future.

Moreover, to be in a state of revolt is to show a true awareness of what it is to be human. When we consider what men might be, the potentialities and possibilities that are in them, in each of us, and that every man, woman and child is one of *us*, and relate this awareness to the actual state and opportunities of so many of us, then the present situation is intolerable. This is a very just and prophetic way of expressing the judgment of man's future upon our present living. And the threat, possibility or occurrence of violence sharply and realistically reminds us that to tolerate the intolerable is to provoke the intolerable.

Humanly speaking, why should the oppressed suffer rather than the oppressors? Why should the deprived suffer rather than the indifferent affluent? Not that the protesters or the offerers and promoters of overt violence are any more likely to do right for right reasons than the acquiescent, the defensive or the explicit or implicit promoters of the oppressions and inequalities of the *status quo*. We are all men and we all (in our 'fallen' or 'sinful' way) prefer to promote righteousness on our own terms rather than to face the cost of attending to, suffering with and working for, what is actually there in the human situation. But protest and violence remind us of the urgency of our responsibility for a human future to be worked out in practical relation to the human possibilities and the inhuman realities of the present. Now is the time to suffer for the removal of the sufferings of men.

Since the future is God's future and the hope of the future is love, we have to see that our human responsibility to contribute is not the same as, nor does it any way imply, any human expectation to control. Man is manifestly not the master of his fate. Or alternatively, if he is, his fate is absurdity. Neither the evidence of my ears and my eyes nor the encouragement of my Christian faith leads me to expect that men will produce utopia. And even if 'they' did, how many men would be fulfilled by it? If there is any state, condition or kingdom fulfilling men in a fully human way, embracing and fulfilling all human living, which includes the living of all humans, then it is the Kingdom of God. But once we are freed from the illusion of control and the mirage of utopia, we can face realistically the responsibility of contribution and we can face hopefully the demand for fighting constantly against imperfections, failures and dissatisfactions. Here man certainly does not have, and certainly will never have, any 'abiding city'. But it is here that we discover the responses and the responsibility of love in constantly rebuilding the city of man in the sure and certain hope of the city of God – which will be one and the same in God's future.

In practice this will have to do with that 'expanding of the threshold' of love and of humanness to which I referred at p. 101 above. Particular problems, decisions and aims, whether they have a short-term or longer-term dimension, all need to be constantly reviewed and kept in this perspective. The fulfilment of man is not a function of housing, economic growth, pharmacological handling of moods, educational diversification or of anything else of which one could think; nor of all of them in combination. Every technical, scientific and operational problem or decision, if it is to be truly human, has to be seen in its proper role as being functional for the human and the human is to do with the mutual extension of love. This is why so much 'human engineering' can be quite irrelevant when it is not harmful. Information, know-how and 'getting things done' are great refuges for human beings who are not yet human enough even to face the fact that they are running away from their own and everyone else's humanity.

However, information, know-how and getting things done are not to be run away from either. Rather they are to be placed and used within the struggle to discern and develop a more truly human context and content. This, I suggest, is how we should attempt to see and handle all the problems we have seen looming up about such matters as biological, psychological or social determinism and individual and social subjectivity. The more information we have about our biological make-up, psychological dynamics or sociological interactions, the more we shall be able to correlate this information with states and possibilities in individuals and groups. Thus the more know-how we shall have about liberating possibilities or promoting options in individuals and groups. The knowledge about correlations (e.g., *this* genetic pattern produces *this* sort of man) can always be used for reductionist purposes. That is to say, it will always be possible to argue in the form 'men (or certain types of men) are *nothing but* the biological elements, psychological forces etc. which can be correlated with a certain character, characteristic or behaviour'. But we can now be quite clear that this will always be an evasion of responsibilities and possibilities and that the debate about the ways in which human beings are determined is really a secondary debate (see p. 90) about how we are to understand our make-up and situation in order to play a creative part in them. It will always look as if men can be reduced in this way because they are emergent in this way. We need one another to become what we might be. Someone who supplies me with a vital physical need (e.g., makes up a hormone deficiency) or removes a crippling psychological block (whether psychoanalytically or pharmacologically) is serving me out of the creativity of the world which is such that it has thrown up men who can and must now help to create one another. For myself, I do not doubt that this is a foretaste of the Kingdom of God wherein we shall all be perfected through the perfections of one another.

Of course, just as such knowledge can be abused in an inhuman way for reductionist purposes, so such know-how can be abused in an inhuman way, not for increasing creativity and freedom among all men (i.e., for extending the threshold of humanness and love), but for establishing the domination and manipulation of some men. Creativity is a battle and the work of love is a constant struggle. The risk of such emerging and co-operating freedom and creativity is immense. We can remain trapped, we can even choose to remain trapped, in the limitations of the subjectivity of our individuality or a group identity which is not yet fully personal, i.e., truly open to loving relationships with other men and with God. Indeed, the situation of not yet being loving persons is the situation of all of us. We are emerging as such or we have the opportunity of emerging as such. But we take these opportunities only as we respond to that which again and again breaks in upon the barriers we seek either to erect or to maintain around our unfinished individual identities and our insufficiently communal and personal groups. By the mercy of God we are not left alone. Change is a constant feature of our environment, including the change of death. One way or another we have to face newness or receive newness. It is a measure of our 'fallenness' that opportunities to extend into newness so often take on the appearance of threats and causes of fear. It is a measure of the love of God, and therefore, of our hope of ultimate fully human newness, that the form of God in the world was that of a man threatened, feared and rejected to death.

We may and must look, therefore, always for the expansion of the threshold of love, the extension of the boundaries of open relationship, mutual sharing and creative care.

There is one human 'problem area' which needs, almost above all, to be seen in this light, at the present stage of our existence. It is a measure of the absurdity of an attempt to write a book about 'man' and the arbitrary choices thereby imposed by length and by the limitations of the author that in this book I have nowhere discussed the relationship between men and women. This is all the more absurd in that sexual relationships are clearly among the most important, powerful, potentially intimate and deeply loving of all human relationships (if not *the* most important). Further, all of us learn our most basic lesson about love and relationship not by words, information or reflection but by our life-giving physical contacts with our mothers. If we are really in touch with the possibilities of love the beginnings of this possibility lay for us in the touch of our mother. Moreover, no one is born for whatever human possibilities there are or will be without the actual physical suffering of a woman.

I have already explained that I decided to write this book from the starting point of the possibilities and threats of our human capacity for science and to extend more broadly into the human situation from there. I still think this is reasonable, in view of the at least superficial dominance which science has over the present human situation. But it is one more piece of evidence about the ambiguity and even contradiction of our situation that such a starting-point can easily lead us to leave out of account, or at least gravely to discount, the basically human things and the fundamental presuppositions of our existence. Women are so vital with regard to the creativity of human living that it is quite possible to discuss the question 'What is man?' at great length without even giving them a separate mention. In this, they are perhaps more godlike than their male opposite numbers, for God also is strangely self-effacing. (A very feminine 'Father-figure'? In reality, love beyond all imagining!)

In any case, the position of women in relation to men certainly provides much evidence of the ambiguities and contradictions of our developing humanity, just as does the whole field of relationships between men and women. In most (if not all?) cultures and societies a woman is underprivileged compared to a man, although what equality between men and women would really mean in relation to a full expression of the femininity of women and the masculinity of men is not at all clear. Further, sex and sexuality is the sphere of the most bewildering range of human possibilities and perversities, extending from the most ecstatic enjoyment of total personal abandonment in personal sharing to the grossest obscenities of exploitation and impersonal use.

When we consider the matter in the context of our attempt to understand man as the emergent collaborator with and sharer in the creative love of God, it would seem that obsession with sexuality is as inhuman as the suppression of sexuality. Here are possibilities to be enjoyed and developed in the whole context of emerging personality and humanity and with regard to the extension of the threshold of love. Until we have worked through and been saved from obsession with sexuality, women cannot possibly be set free to be fully persons rather than sexual objects. However, there is clearly no hope of being freed from this obsession until we are liberated to enjoy sexuality in a personal and human way. Meanwhile we have to face in a positive way all the present confusions, whether they are about 'permissiveness', pornography and eroticism, or about those true possibilities of love which will promote truly personal freedom, liberation from shame and a really human erotic enjoyment which is neither exploitive, obsessive nor isolated from the whole range of personal responsibilities and potentialities. Nowhere is it more necessary than here to be clear that we have the opportunity of sharing in the creative and costly struggle of love to find a way through present human limitation and selfishness to the building up of relationships and situations which promote an identity and a community which is always expanding in both care and enjoyment.

We shall never be enabled to deal creatively with sin in the field of human sexuality or in any other field of human failure and achievement unless we also receive a glimpse of the glory which is given for our enjoyment, and at work for our fulfilment. The antidote to sin is not duty but praise.

For duty is to do with our efforts. But praise is to do with the simple existence of goodness. This is where no amount of information, however accurate and important, can be any substitute for experience. It is also why the most uninformed man, woman or child can be far more human and far more open to what is involved and offered in being human than any committee of the best informed men and women in the world, either individually or collectively. For consider – can you imagine *any* answer to the question 'What is man?' which would satisfy you? What are we looking for when we ask this question? (cf. Chapter 1). Surely not, in the last analysis, information which either drives the mind to further questions and search for further information or else stupefies the mind with the impossibility of facing the rapidly multiplying questions. Rather, we are looking for experience in which we can rest while we live and be completely alive while we rest. We shall know the final answer to the question 'What is man?' when we are in the living presence of, and are a living part of, that which causes us to say only 'it is good for us to be here'.

Information we need and must have for all our actions and decisions both with regard to the moving patterns of our individual and social lives and with regard to the threats and possibilities developing in and for human beings all around us and into the temporal future. There are endless things to be done, developed and challenged in the name of our actual and potential common humanity. But doing is evidence only *that* we exist and is aimed at *enabling* us to exist. Being is *how* we exist and doing is not worth doing unless there is something worth watching, sharing and being. Indeed, the escape of activity is one of the easiest and most dangerous ways of escaping from the responsibilities and opportunities both of being ourselves and towards the human being of other people. *Doing* good is such a useless and joyless activity, especially if it is the professed centre and purpose of our individual organizational or corporate lives. For who are we to do good and what is good that we may do it? And what good will it be when it is done?

Thus, to live as man, to live up to and out of the depth, possibilities and mysteries which are reflected in the question 'What is man?', we must be concerned to receive a living, creative, sustaining and delicate balance between our responsibilities for causing to be and our opportunities for letting be. Love has to be received before it can be properly enjoyed or returned. Life has to be entered into before it can be lived out of. We are not on our own and we are not yet ourselves. On our own we can neither be ourselves nor build ourselves. Such is the Christian understanding and hope. Thus man is to be understood as a receiver of the possibilities of life but an active receiver, a responder to the offers and opportunities of love but a creative responder, a constructor of situations, persons and societies which overcome limitation and evil and liberate growth and goodness, but a dependent constructor. What he receives, what he searches for, what he builds up and what he enjoys is the image of himself in God.

But this not a narcissistic search or enjoyment. For the God who offers him the divine image so that he can be truly human is the God who is love and the God whose human embodiment is Jesus. Thus the ultimate shape which is offered is a shape which embraces the mutual fulfilment of all things through the particular fulfilment of each. I shall be me in such a way that I receive all that I am from all things without interruption or interference, and this being of mine I shall receive because I have been brought to the point and place where I am free to give myself uninterruptedly to all things. Hence it will be good to be there, good beyond either belief or question.

Then we shall know what is the worth of worth and what the final meaning of worship. Meanwhile, we have our human calling to receive all existence as basically worshipful and to be co-operators with God in promoting the emergence of that which is endlessly worshipful. In the pursuit of this calling we are to discover our own shape, worship and worth. Worship and love, love and worship, are focused in experience, not in information, but they are the means and modes of glorifying all true information, that is to say of discerning in this information or that, some glory to be enjoyed and some glory to be promoted. Neither the world, nor our own experience, nor any light we can draw from biblical faith and from Jesus Christ, suggest that this can possibly be done without cost. Hence it is from praise and from suffering, from worship and from compassion, from enjoyment and from the bitterness of human faces marred by inhumanity, that we may hope to pursue, in both action and contemplation, the answer to the question 'What is man?'. And what we seek, although we do not know what we seek, we may hope to find. For our destination is our fellow traveller and our fellow sufferer, the God and Father of Jesus Christ.

Clearly it is blasphemy to define man. But a way to regard him from which much might flow is to see him, to see all of us, to see myself, as the potential worshipper who has the capacity to fall in love.

For Further Reading

To get the flavour of the open scientific situation with regard to man:

Beyond Reductionism, (The Alpbach Symposium), ed. A. Koestler and J. R. Smythies, Hutchinson, 1969.

The Living Stream, Sir A. Hardy, Collins, 1965.

The Divine Flame, Sir A. Hardy, Collins, 1966.

The Ethical Animal, C. H. Waddington, Allen & Unwin, 1960.

To get the flavour of the possibilities and relevance of the Christian faith and tradition:

Grace and Personality, J. Oman, Collins (Fontana), 1960.

The Nature and Destiny of Man, R. Niebuhr, Nisbet, 1941–3.

Amor Dei, J. Burnaby, Hodder & Stoughton, 1938.

Evil and the God of Love, J. Hick, Macmillan, 1966.